The Best Pasta Cookbook:

100 Classic Pasta Recipes

Bonnie Scott

BONNIE SCOTT

PASTA RECIPES

PASTA & SAUCES — 13

CHICKEN & MEAT PASTAS — 35

SEAFOOD PASTAS   94

VEGGIE PASTAS — 113

PASTA SOUPS — 131

SALADS & SIDES 146

HEALTHY SUBSTITUTIONS FOR CANNED SOUP 159

PASTA RECIPES

With so many shapes and sizes available, it's easy to create a tasty and wholesome meal featuring pasta. It's a perfect neutral canvas to combine with your favorite ingredients and seasonings. With over 300 shapes, you can easily vary your presentation, and when you're strapped for time, you can make a complete meal in as little as 30 minutes.

Your meals can be hearty and comforting when the weather's cold or light and fresh when the temperature soars. Pasta is a great showcase for seasonal fresh ingredients and can stretch costly ingredients for a meal to feed a crowd.

Some pasta recipes are all-in-one dishes that require only a simple side dish to complete your meal. Recipes that may be a bit more involved can be assembled in advance and reheated or served at room temperature.

As much as we love pasta, it's gotten a bad reputation over the years. Some detractors claim it's fattening, that it's merely empty calories, that it elevates sugar or sodium levels. However, as a savvy cook, you can make your favorite pasta dish a healthy and nutritious meal that's fit for everyone in your family.

Tips for Making Your Pasta Recipes Healthier

The USDA states that carbohydrates, such as pasta, play an important role in a healthy diet. That's why in their 2015 - 2020 Dietary Guidelines for Americans, the USDA recommends consuming 45% to 65% of your total calories from these types of nutrients. At least half of this amount should be whole grains.

There are lots of ways you can pare down the calories and bulk up the nutritional level of any pasta dish. By simply adding a few of these ideas, you'll be serving your family healthier meals, and they probably won't even notice!

Give vegetable-based or whole-wheat pasta a try.

Vegetable-based pasta is made with the same type of flour but has puréed tomato, spinach, carrots and zucchini added for extra vitamins.

Whole-wheat pasta adds fiber to your diet. That fiber causes your body to digest your meal slowly. Your body maintains a steadier glucose level, which means you'll feel full longer. However, whole-wheat pasta does have a different flavor than white flour pasta.

You may find that whole-wheat pasta just doesn't cut it with some recipes. Its nutty flavor pairs well with strong-flavored pesto sauce. It also works well with roasted vegetables like squash or cauliflower and root vegetables. Hearty casseroles are also good choices for fortified whole-wheat pasta.

Cook pasta al dente.

Your digestive enzymes take longer to break down starch into sugar when pasta is slightly undercooked. In this way, they are released more slowly into the blood stream, and you'll feel full longer.

Start checking your pasta two to three minutes before the manufacturer's recommended cooking time. Also, drain your pasta immediately, as it will continue to cook in the hot water.

Swap out flour noodles with veggie noodles.

If you're trying to cut down on carbs and calories, swap out your flour-based noodles with veggie noodles. These noodle substitutes have minimal calories and can hold as much sauce as any standard pasta.

Using a vegetable peeler or spiralizer, cut your choice of veggie into noodles. Sauté with a dab of olive or canola oil to soften, and add your favorite sauce and seasonings. Parsnips, carrots, zucchini and butternut squash are all potentials for tasty veggie noodles. Spaghetti squash is also a popular choice for trimmed-down, health-conscious pasta recipes.

Portion control is a no-brainer.

The larger the portion, the more calories on your plate. You may be surprised that in Italy, the average serving size of pasta is nearly half the size of what we typically serve in the United States. American cooks normally serve almost four ounces of pasta, while Italians may serve approximately 2.5 ounces or less.

While we may consider the pasta course the entire meal, Italian diners are eating pasta as only one of several courses.

Add side dishes of vegetables when serving pasta.

Begin your meal with a green salad and serve sides of roasted, steamed or sautéed vegetables. Add extra portions of vegetables to your recipes. Add enough, so the main ingredients become the vegetables, and the protein and pasta become secondary.

Make meat a condiment.

If meat is a main component of your dish, make sure it's as lean as you can. Purchase the leanest ground beef or opt for ground turkey for your sauce or meatballs. Use turkey or chicken sausage instead of pork sausage.

In many parts of the world, meat is very expensive. Cooks use meat as a condiment, not the focal point of a dish. Try adding less meat than is called for in a recipe. Increase bulk with extra mushrooms, or other vegetables. With strong-flavored meats like bacon, ham and other cured meats, it only takes a little bit to add that extra pizzazz to your dish.

Go meatless a few times a week. A light marinara sauce or a bit of olive oil, lemon, and grated cheese makes a welcome change to heavy, robust meals.

Use healthy options when choosing a sauce.

If you're going to use commercially canned sauces, read the labels. You need to look for one that has three grams of fat or less, a maximum of 75 calories and no more than 150 mg sodium per serving.

Cream sauces are generally high in all those departments, so a tomato-based product should be your go-to sauce. Tomato-based pasta sauce can be really easy to make, so you have total control over your fat, calorie and sodium intake.

There's nothing more decadent than a rich, buttery cream sauce.

However, it's probably not one you should have on your short list of everyday go-to recipes. If you're bound and determined to make a creamy sauce, today's dairy aisles have lots of low-calorie substitutes.

Reduced fat cheeses, creams and yogurt can be used in place of the yummy, high-calorie versions. However, by giving up that wonderful, creamy goodness, you may be changing the texture and/or rich flavor of your recipe.

If you're going to 'go low' and use low fat or fat-free versions, be prepared to taste a difference. If it's one you and your family can live with, that's great.

Sometimes a low-fat version is acceptable, while other times you just can't beat the luxury of a 'heart attack on a plate' version. Just remember, 'portion control.'

Add cheese as a garnish.

Many recipes call for cheese to be added directly to the sauce, so all the cheesy goodness blends in. Instead of adding loads of cheese (and fat and calories) into your sauce, just spoon a bit on top of each serving. That way, you'll get a fresh, undiluted taste of cheese with every bite.

Pasta & Sauces

Summer Pasta with Pesto

4 servings

INGREDIENTS

2 tablespoons butter
1 small onion, minced
1/2 lb. cooked ham, julienned
1/2 lb. tiny peas, cooked
4 to 6 small new potatoes, peeled, cooked, and halved
1 cup pesto sauce
1 lb. fettuccine
Parmesan cheese

PREPARATION

Melt butter in a large skillet and sauté onion over medium heat for 5 minutes. Add ham, peas, potatoes and pesto sauce to skillet; heat through.

Cook fettuccine according to package directions; drain. Place hot pasta in a large, heated serving bowl. Add the potato-pesto mixture and toss gently to mix. Sprinkle with Parmesan cheese and serve.

Mediterranean Pasta

4 servings

INGREDIENTS

6 oz. mostaccioli
1 (10 oz.) package frozen chopped spinach or 1 pkg.
frozen artichoke hearts
8 slices bacon, coarsely chopped
3 cloves garlic, minced
1 (16 oz.) can whole tomatoes, in juice, undrained,
coarsely chopped
1/2 teaspoon salt, to taste
1/8 to 1/4 teaspoon crushed red pepper
1/2 cup ripe olives, sliced

PREPARATION

Cook pasta according to package directions; drain.

Thaw and drain spinach (or artichoke hearts).

Cook bacon until crisp; remove all but 1 tablespoon drippings. Add garlic; sauté for 30 seconds. Add spinach or artichoke hearts, cook 3 minutes. Add tomatoes, salt and crushed red pepper, stirring occasionally. Cook for 5 minutes. Add olives, cook for 3 minutes. Toss with mostaccioli.

Italian Spaghetti Sauce

4 servings

INGREDIENTS

3/4 cup onion, chopped
1 clove garlic, minced
3 tablespoons vegetable or olive oil
2 (1 lb. each) cans, or 4 cups tomatoes, cut up
2 (6 oz. each) tomato paste
2 cups water
1 teaspoon brown sugar
1 1/2 teaspoons salt
1/2 teaspoon black pepper
1 1/2 teaspoons dried oregano
1 bay leaf
1 (16 oz.) pkg. spaghetti

PREPARATION

Sauté onion and garlic in oil until tender, but not brown. Add tomatoes, tomato paste, water, brown sugar, salt, pepper, oregano and bay leaf; simmer uncovered 1 hour. If adding meatballs, add after 1/2 hour of simmering.

Cook spaghetti according to package directions; drain. Discard bay leaf and serve sauce over spaghetti.

Cheese Ravioli

4 servings

INGREDIENTS

To make 3/4 lb. of noodles:
1 to 1-1/2 cups flour
1 egg
1 egg white
1 tablespoon olive oil
1 teaspoon salt
Few drops of water

Cheese filling:
1 1/2 lb. ricotta cheese
3/4 cup Romano cheese, grated
2 teaspoon onion, grated
3 egg yolks
1 1/2 teaspoons salt

PREPARATION

Pour flour in a large mixing bowl or in a pile on pastry board; create a well in center of flour. Place egg, egg white, oil and salt in the well; mix with a fork or fingers until dough can be gathered into a ball. Moisten any remaining dry pieces of flour with drops of water; press into the ball.

In a medium bowl, combine ricotta cheese, Romano cheese, onion, egg yolks and salt. Carefully stir together until well mixed. Set aside until dough is rolled out.

Separate dough into 4 pieces; roll one piece as thin as possible. Cover rolled pasta with damp towel to prevent drying. Roll out second piece of dough to same size and shape; place 1 tablespoon cheese mixture every 2 inches on the pasta, across and down.

Dip pastry brush or index finger in water. Make vertical and horizontal lines between the mounds of filling. Use enough water to wet lines evenly, as water acts to bond finished ravioli together.

Carefully spread second sheet of rolled-out pasta on top of first, pressing down firmly around filling along wet lines. Using a ravioli cutter, pastry wheel or small knife, cut pasta into squares along wetted lines. Separate mounds and set them aside on waxed paper.

Roll out and prepare other portions of dough similarly.

To cook, drop pasta into 6 to 8 quarts rapidly boiling, salted water and stir gently with wooden spoon to keep pasta from sticking to one another or going to the bottom of the pan. Boil about 8 minutes, until tender. Drain thoroughly in large sieve.

Serve with tomato sauce or add butter and freshly-grated Romano cheese and gently stir all together immediately before serving.

Penne Rigate with Red Bell Pepper Sauce

4 servings

INGREDIENTS

3/4 lb. penne rigate
4 oz. olive oil, extra-virgin
1 large Spanish onion, julienned
2 large red bell peppers, julienned
1 tablespoon capers, drained
1/2 teaspoon dried pepper flakes
4 oz. red wine vinegar
1 (8 oz.) can tomato sauce
Salt and pepper to taste
2 tablespoons fresh basil, shredded
Pecorino cheese, freshly grated

PREPARATION

Cook pasta according to package directions; drain, reserving 3/4 cup of cooking water.

Sauté onion in olive oil until just starting to brown. Add bell pepper, capers, pepper flakes, salt and pepper; cook until peppers are softened with light brown spots, about 10 minutes. Add vinegar and simmer until liquid evaporates. Mix in tomato sauce and cook 5 minutes.

Add pasta and reserved water to the sauce. Stirring occasionally, simmer to desired thickness, about 2 minutes. Stir in basil. Garnish individual servings with Pecorino cheese.

Cheese Manicotti

4 to 6 servings

INGREDIENTS

1 (8 oz.) pkg. manicotti

Sauce:

1 (14.5 oz.) can tomatoes
1 (6 oz.) can tomato paste
6 oz. red wine
1 onion, sautéed
1 garlic clove
1 bay leaf
1/2 teaspoon granulated sugar
1/2 teaspoon salt
1/2 to 1 teaspoon each of oregano or basil

Filling:

1 lb. Ricotta cheese
1/4 lb. Prosciutto (or cooked chopped spinach or omit)
1 cup reduced fat mozzarella or Jack cheese, shredded
2 eggs, lightly beaten
1/2 cup Parmesan cheese
Salt and pepper

PREPARATION

Cook pasta according to package directions; drain.

Combine all sauce ingredients in a medium saucepan; simmer 30 to 60 minutes.

In a large bowl, combine all filling ingredients; mix well.

To Assemble:

Fill manicotti with filling mixture. Place in single layer in baking dish. Cover with sauce and extra Parmesan cheese. Bake at 350 degrees F. for 15 minutes, covered, and 15 minutes uncovered.

Aglie-Olio (Garlic and Oil)

4 servings

INGREDIENTS

1/4 lb. linguine or bow tie pasta
2 tablespoons butter
2 tablespoons olive oil
2 cloves garlic
1/2 red pepper, seeded
Parmesan or Romano cheese
Black pepper to taste

PREPARATION

Cook pasta according to package directions; drain; do not rinse.

Oil mixture:
In butter and oil, simmer crushed garlic and pepper pod while pasta cooks; discard pepper pod and garlic. Pour over pasta. Garnish with cheese and black pepper.

Linguine Carbonara

4 servings

INGREDIENTS

2 tablespoons butter
1/2 cup onion, chopped
1 tablespoon shallot, minced
1/4 lb. bacon, chopped
1/4 cup dry white wine
3 eggs, beaten
1/2 cup Parmesan cheese, freshly grated
1/2 teaspoon pepper
2 tablespoons fresh parsley, chopped
1 pound linguine

PREPARATION

Sauté onion, shallot and bacon in butter for 5 minutes or until bacon is browned. Add wine and simmer uncovered, until wine evaporates.

In a medium bowl, whisk eggs, cheese, pepper and parsley.

Cook pasta according to package directions; drain. Place pasta in a heated serving bowl and toss with egg mixture. Pour on bacon mix and toss. Serve while hot.

Linguine with Spring Vegetables

6 to 8 servings

INGREDIENTS

2 tablespoons light olive oil
1/2 cup unsalted butter
1 medium onion, minced
2 large cloves garlic, minced
1/2 lb. mushrooms, thinly sliced
1 medium zucchini, thinly sliced
1 medium carrot, julienned
1 lb. fresh asparagus, sliced diagonally
1 cup heavy cream
1/2 cup chicken stock*
3 green onions with tops, thinly sliced
1 cup broccoli florets, chopped
1/4 cup fresh basil, chopped, or 3 teaspoons dried basil
Salt and black pepper to taste
1 pound linguine
1/2 cup freshly grated Parmesan cheese
1/4 cup minced fresh parsley

PREPARATION

Sauté onion and garlic in olive oil and butter in a large saucepan until soft. Add mushrooms, zucchini, carrots and asparagus; cook 2 to 3 minutes. Add heavy cream and chicken stock; cook until liquid is reduced. Add green onions, broccoli, and basil. Season with salt and pepper.

Cook pasta according to package directions; drain. Add vegetables to pasta and toss with cheese to coat. Garnish with parsley.

Chicken stock/broth recipe page 164

Rigatoni with Shiitakes and Artichokes

6 servings

INGREDIENTS

1 (16 oz.) pkg. rigatoni
3 tablespoons olive oil
1/3 cup shallots, finely chopped
2 red bell peppers, cut into strips
8 oz. shiitake mushrooms
1 tablespoon garlic, chopped
1 1/4 cups chicken broth*
1 (14 oz.) can artichoke hearts, drained and quartered
1 teaspoon grated lemon zest
3 tablespoons lemon juice
1 teaspoon salt
1/4 teaspoon hot red pepper flakes
1/4 teaspoon black pepper
2 tablespoons parsley, chopped
1 cup Romano or Parmesan cheese, grated

PREPARATION

Cook the rigatoni according to package directions; drain.

Sauté shallots in olive oil for 1 minute or until browned. Add bell peppers and shiitake mushrooms; cook for 10 minutes or vegetables are tender, stirring occasionally. Add garlic; cook 1 minute.

Add chicken broth, artichokes, lemon zest and juice, salt, hot red pepper flakes and black pepper to mushrooms; bring to a boil. Reduce heat and simmer 5 minutes. Stir in parsley. Toss hot rigatoni with mushroom mixture and shredded Romano in a large bowl.

Chicken stock/broth recipe page 164

Tortellini Alfredo

2 servings

INGREDIENTS

8 oz. tortellini
1 teaspoon butter
1/2 teaspoon shallots, chopped
1 oz. prosciutto, diced
1 oz. fresh mushrooms, sliced
1/8 teaspoon nutmeg
3 oz. chicken stock
6 oz. heavy cream
Parmesan cheese
Fresh parsley, chopped

PREPARATION

Cook pasta according to directions on package; drain.

In a large skillet, melt butter and sauté shallots. Add prosciutto and mushrooms; sauté until golden. Add nutmeg, chicken stock, cream and drained tortellini; simmer until sauce thickens.

Serve sauce over pasta and garnish Parmesan cheese and parsley.

Fettuccine with Gorgonzola

6 servings

INGREDIENTS

1/2 lb. fresh spinach
1 cup heavy cream
3 oz. Gorgonzola cheese, grated
4 tablespoons butter
1 oz. vodka
Salt and pepper
1/4 lb. reduced fat ricotta cheese, grated
1 lb. fettuccine
3 oz. shredded Parmesan cheese

PREPARATION

Wash spinach and shake to remove excess water. Cook spinach in the water clinging to the leaves; drain and chop.

In a saucepan, bring cream to a simmer. Add Gorgonzola cheese, butter and vodka. Blend; add salt and pepper to taste. Add spinach and ricotta; simmer and stir until blended.

Cook noodles according to package directions; drain. Pour sauce over noodles and toss to coat. Sprinkle with Parmesan cheese and toss again. Serve immediately.

Fettuccine with Wilted Escarole and Mushrooms

4 servings

INGREDIENTS

3/4 lb. fettuccine
1/4 cup olive oil
4 garlic cloves, thinly sliced
1/2 teaspoon red pepper, crushed
1 1/2 (5 oz.) cup mushrooms, thinly sliced
Salt and pepper to taste
1 (1/2 lb.) head escarole, cored and cut into 1-inch ribbons
6 tablespoons Parmesan cheese (plus more for serving)

PREPARATION

Cook pasta according to package directions; drain. Reserve 1 cup of cooking water.

Using a large deep skillet, heat olive oil. Add garlic and red pepper. Sauté over medium heat 30 seconds, until fragrant but not browned. Add mushrooms and season with salt and pepper. Cook about 5 minutes, until vegetables soften and begin to brown. Add escarole and cook until wilted.

Add pasta along with reserved cooking water and heat until the sauce is slightly thickened, about 2 minutes. Season with salt and pepper as needed. Add Parmesan cheese and toss to coat.

Fettuccine Alfredo

4 to 6 servings

INGREDIENTS

1 (8 oz.) pkg. fettuccine
5 tablespoons butter, melted
1/2 teaspoon sage
1/2 teaspoon basil
1/4 teaspoon garlic salt
1/8 teaspoon white pepper
1/2 pint heavy cream
1/2 cup Swiss cheese, grated
3/4 cup Parmesan cheese, grated

PREPARATION

Cook noodles according to package directions; drain.

Mix sage, basil, garlic salt and pepper with melted butter. Mix with warm noodles. Blend in cream and cheeses. Toss until cheese is melted.

Pesto Spaghetti

4 to 6 servings

INGREDIENTS

8 oz. spaghetti
1 cup fresh basil leaves
1/4 cup fresh parsley leaves
1/4 cup olive oil
1 clove garlic
1/2 teaspoon salt
1/4 cup fresh grated Parmesan cheese
2 tablespoons toasted pine nuts

PREPARATION

Cook spaghetti according to package directions; drain.

Place basil leaves, parsley, olive oil, garlic and salt into a food processor. Blend until smooth and stir in Parmesan cheese. Stir the pesto into hot pasta. Sprinkle with pine nuts.

Spaghetti Casserole

4 servings

INGREDIENTS

1 (10.5 oz.) can low fat cream of mushroom soup*
2 cups low fat milk
1/2 teaspoon granulated sugar
Salt and pepper to taste
1 (12 oz.) pkg. spaghetti
1 pint reduced fat sour cream
1 onion, minced
1 lb. Cheddar cheese, shredded
1 cup round butter crackers, crushed
8 oz. margarine

PREPARATION

Blend soup, milk, sugar, salt and pepper. Cover pasta with water. Bringing water to a boil, remove from heat and let stand 10 minutes, until soft. Layer spaghetti, sour cream, onions and Cheddar cheese in a 13x9-inch baking dish and repeat. Pour soup over mixture in baking dish. *(*or use mushroom soup recipe page 162)*

Sauté crackers in butter until lightly browned and distribute evenly over top of casserole. Bake at 325 degrees F. until bubbly, about 60 minutes.

Chicken & Meat Pastas

Corn Chowder Casserole

4 servings

INGREDIENTS

1 lb. lean ground beef
1/2 cup onion, finely diced
3 cups elbow macaroni
1/2 cup American cheese, shredded
2 cups cream corn
1 teaspoon salt
1/2 teaspoon black pepper
Non-stick cooking spray

PREPARATION

Brown ground beef and onion together; drain grease. Cook pasta according to package directions; drain. Add cheese, corn, salt and pepper to macaroni. Blend well and add meat mixture. Spray a baking dish with non-stick cooking spray; add mixture. Bake at 350 degrees F. for 20 to 30 minutes.

Italian Ziti Medley

2 to 3 servings

INGREDIENTS

1/2 lb. ziti
1/2 lb. sliced Italian sausage
1/2 cup butter or margarine
1 cup green bell pepper strips
1 cup mushrooms, sliced
1/3 cup onion, chopped
1/3 cup flour
2 1/4 cups low fat milk
2 cups (8 oz.) Cheddar cheese, shredded, divided
1/2 cup Parmesan cheese, grated
1/2 teaspoon black pepper

PREPARATION

Cook ziti according to package directions; drain

In Dutch oven, brown sausage. Remove meat with slotted spoon and discard grease from pan. Set aside.

In the same pan, sauté bell peppers, mushrooms and onion in butter until soft; whisk in flour and slowly incorporate milk. Continue stirring until mixture thickens. Add Parmesan cheese and 1 1/2 cups Cheddar cheese; stir until melted and smooth.

Stir ziti and sausage into vegetable-cheese mixture. Place in baking dish and top with remaining Cheddar cheese. Bake at 350 degrees F. for 30 minutes.

Orzo with Braised Short Ribs in Burgundy Sauce

4 servings

INGREDIENTS

4 lb. beef short ribs
1/2 cup vegetable oil
1/2 cup flour
Salt and pepper to taste
4 stalks celery, coarsely chopped
2 carrots, coarsely chopped
1 large onion, coarsely chopped
1/8 teaspoon thyme
2 bay leaves
5 cloves garlic
1 (29 oz.) can of tomato puree
1/2 bottle burgundy wine
4 tablespoons cornstarch, mixed with 1/2 cup water
1 lb. orzo pasta

PREPARATION

Heat vegetable oil in Dutch oven until hot. Toss short ribs in flour seasoned with pepper and salt and place in pre-heated pan; brown well on all sides. Add celery, carrots, onion, thyme, bay leaves and garlic. Add tomato puree, burgundy wine and enough water to cover meat and vegetables.

Heat pot to boiling; Reduce heat, cover and simmer for 1 1/2 hours. Remove ribs and strain liquid; return sauce to pan and simmer until sauce is reduced by 1/3. Thicken with cornstarch and keep warm.

Cook pasta according to package directions; drain. Place pasta on individual plates, top with ribs and sauce.

Turkey Chili Macaroni

8 servings

INGREDIENTS

1 1/4 lb. ground turkey
2 tablespoons olive oil
1 medium onion, chopped
1 cup green bell pepper or celery, chopped
2 1/2 cups chicken broth*
7 oz. macaroni
1 (15 oz.) can tomato sauce
2 tablespoons vinegar
1 1/2 teaspoon granulated sugar
1 teaspoon chili powder
1 teaspoon garlic salt
6 tablespoons grated Parmesan cheese, divided
1 1/2 tablespoons parsley, snipped

PREPARATION

Heat oil in a Dutch oven; sauté ground turkey, onion and green bell pepper or celery until meat is no longer pink. Remove mixture from pan, reserving juices. Add broth to pan; bring to a boil.

Add uncooked macaroni and simmer 10 minutes, stirring often, until broth mostly absorbed. Add tomato sauce, vinegar, sugar, chili powder, garlic salt and 4 tablespoons of Parmesan cheese. Simmer 10 minutes. Garnish individual portions with Parmesan cheese and parsley.

Chicken stock/broth recipe page 164

Skillet Pasta with Sausage & Vegetables

6 to 8 servings

INGREDIENTS

2 cups rotini
1 lb. spicy Italian sausage, sliced
1/2 cup onions, chopped
1 1/2 cups zucchini, sliced
1/2 cup carrots, sliced
1/2 cup cut bell peppers, julienned
2 cups cherry tomatoes, halved
1 teaspoon basil leaves
1/2 teaspoon salt
1/8 teaspoon black pepper
1/2 cup red wine (optional)

PREPARATION

Cook pasta according to package directions; drain.

Sauté sausage, onions, zucchini, carrots, bell peppers, tomatoes, basil leaves, salt and pepper until vegetables are tender-crisp. Add wine and cook briefly to evaporate liquid. Mix in pasta. Garnish individual portions with Parmesan cheese.

Pasta "Roman Style"

4 servings

INGREDIENTS

3 to 5 tablespoons olive oil
1 medium to small onion, minced
1 clove of garlic, minced
1/4 to 1/3 lb. pancetta*, diced fine
2 (14.5 oz. each) cans whole tomatoes, chopped
1/8 teaspoon red pepper flakes
1 (16 oz.) pkg. bucatini, linguine or rigatoni pasta
1/4 to 1/3 cup Parmesan or Romano cheese, shredded

PREPARATION

Cook pasta according to package directions; drain.

In a large skillet, sauté onion and garlic in oil until onion is translucent. In a separate skillet, cook pancetta until it is browned and some of the fat is rendered. Add cooked pancetta to the onion-garlic mixture; add tomatoes with juice. Cook uncovered for 10 minutes. Add pepper flakes and adjust seasoning as necessary. Serve over al dente pasta. Add cheese on top before serving.

Pancetta is an unsmoked Italian bacon. Can be purchased at most large grocery stores.

Spaghetti Pie

4 servings

INGREDIENTS

1 cup low fat ricotta cheese or sour cream
1 (6 oz.) pkg. reduced fat shredded mozzarella cheese

Crust:

6 oz. thin spaghetti
1/2 clove garlic, finely diced
1/4 cup butter or margarine
1 egg, lightly beaten
1/2 cup Parmesan cheese
1 teaspoon dried basil or 1 tablespoon fresh basil

Filling:

3/4 lb. Italian sausage, ground
1/2 lb. ground beef
1/2 c. chopped onion
1 (6 oz.) can tomato paste
1 (15 oz.) can tomato sauce
1 teaspoon granulated sugar
1 teaspoon dried basil
1 teaspoon dried oregano
1/4 cup white wine

PREPARATION

Cook spaghetti according to package directions; drain. In a large bowl, combine spaghetti with garlic, butter or margarine, beaten egg, Parmesan cheese and basil. Loosely chop pasta mixture and press into a 10-inch pie plate sprayed with non-stick vegetable spray.

Brown ground sausage, beef and onion; drain. Add tomato paste, tomato sauce, sugar, dried basil, oregano and wine; heat. Spread ricotta cheese or sour cream over crust and top with ground beef mixture. Cover with mozzarella cheese. Bake at 350 degrees F. for 30 minutes.

Baked Ziti

6 servings

INGREDIENTS

8 oz. ziti
2 tablespoons olive oil
1 lb. lean ground beef
1 onion, chopped
2 cloves garlic, peeled and chopped
1 (28 oz.) can crushed tomatoes, undrained
1 (16 oz.) can tomato sauce
Salt and pepper to taste
1 teaspoon oregano
1/2 teaspoon marjoram
1/4 cup chopped parsley
1/4 lb. reduced fat mozzarella cheese, shredded
1/4 cup Parmesan cheese

PREPARATION

Cook ziti according to package directions; drain.

Heat olive oil in saucepan, Add ground beef and onion. Cook until meat is lightly browned. Pour off excess fat. Add garlic, tomatoes with liquid, tomato sauce, salt and pepper, oregano and marjoram. Simmer for 15 minutes.

Mix cooked ziti and sauce together in a 2-1/2 quart casserole dish. Combine mozzarella and Parmesan cheeses; sprinkle over ziti mixture. Sprinkle with chopped parsley. Bake at 350 degrees F. for 25 minutes, or until lightly browned and bubbly.

Gemelli with Sweet Sausage and Spinach

4 servings

INGREDIENTS

3/4 lb. gemelli or penne pasta
2 tablespoons extra-virgin olive oil
1 large onion, quartered lengthwise and thinly sliced
1/2 teaspoon red pepper, crushed
1 lb. bulk sweet Italian sausage
2 cups coarsely chopped baby spinach
1/2 pint red grape tomatoes
1/2 cup freshly grated Parmesan cheese

PREPARATION

Cook pasta according to package directions; drain and reserve some cooking water.

Sauté onion in olive oil in a large saucepan until softened, about 4 to 5 minutes. Add crushed red pepper and sausage. Cook 5 minutes or until meat is no longer pink. Add spinach and tomatoes. Cook until softened, about 3 minutes. Add pasta and a little reserved cooking water to saucepan and cook over medium heat, crushing tomatoes, until heated through, about 2 minutes. Garnish individual bowls with Parmesan cheese.

Terrific Turkey Lasagna

8 servings

INGREDIENTS

6 wide lasagna noodles
1 pkg. (about 1 1/4 lb.) lean ground turkey
1/2 cup onion, chopped
4 cups prepared spaghetti sauce
1 cup low fat ricotta or cottage cheese
4 to 8 oz. low fat mozzarella cheese, sliced
2 tablespoons Parmesan cheese

PREPARATION

Cook noodles according to package directions; drain.

Spray a large skillet with non-stick cooking spray. Crumble ground turkey into skillet. Add onions; cook and stir over medium-high heat for 5 to 7 minutes, or until the turkey is lightly browned. Stir in the spaghetti sauce and simmer over low heat 15 minutes. Reserve 1 cup of meat sauce.

Place 3 noodles in a 13x9-inch baking dish. Top with 2 cups of meat sauce, 1/2 cup of ricotta and 1/2 of the mozzarella cheese. Repeat, topping with reserved meat sauce. Sprinkle with Parmesan cheese. Bake at 350 degrees F. for 30 to 40 minutes or until hot and bubbly.

Ham and Artichoke Lasagna

8 to 10 servings

INGREDIENTS

2 tablespoons olive oil
1 cup carrots, shredded
1 (8 oz.) can mushrooms, sliced
5 green onions, chopped
1/4 cup dry sherry
1/2 cup heavy cream
1 teaspoon basil
2 lb. boneless hickory-smoked ham, cut in 1-inch cubes
2 (14 oz. each) cans artichoke hearts, drained and quartered
1 (24 oz.) container low fat small curd cottage cheese
2 eggs, beaten
1/2 cup (2 oz.) grated Parmesan cheese
8 oz. lasagna noodles
3 cups (12 oz.) reduced fat mozzarella cheese, shredded
Non-stick cooking spray

PREPARATION

In a skillet, heat oil and sauté carrots, mushrooms and onions over moderate heat until tender. Stir in sherry and cook for 2 minutes. Stir in cream and basil; cook for an additional 2 minutes, or until slightly thickened. Remove from heat; stir in ham and artichokes.

In a separate bowl, combine cottage cheese, eggs and Parmesan cheese; mix well.

Cook noodles according to package directions; drain. Layer noodles, ham mixture, cheese mixture and mozzarella cheese in a 9x13-inch baking dish sprayed with non-stick cooking spray. Repeat two more times, ending with mozzarella cheese. Cover and bake at 350 degrees F. for 45 minutes. Uncover and bake for 15 minutes or until cheese is light brown. Let stand for 15 minutes before serving.

Ham Casserole

4 servings

INGREDIENTS

2 cups macaroni
1 1/2 cups green peas frozen
2 tablespoons red pimentos
1 1/4 cups cooked diced ham
1/2 cup sliced mushrooms

Cheese sauce:

6 tablespoons butter
2 teaspoon flour
1 1/2 cups milk
1 cup American cheese, diced

Non-stick cooking spray

PREPARATION

Cook pasta according to directions on package; drain. Combine with peas, pimento, ham and mushrooms.

Cheese Sauce
In a small saucepan, melt butter and stir in flour to make a roux. Slowly add milk, continuing to stir until

mixture thickens. Lower heat, add cheese and stir until cheese melts.

Add Cheese Sauce to the mixture and place in a 9x13-inch baking dish that has been sprayed with non-stick cooking spray. Bake 45 minutes at 350 degrees F. for 25 minutes, or until cheese is bubbly.

Low Calorie Streamlined Lasagna

6 servings

INGREDIENTS

1 tablespoon olive oil
1/3 cup onion, minced
1 lb. lean ground beef
1 clove garlic
3/4 teaspoon salt
1/4 teaspoon black pepper
1/4 teaspoon dried oregano
3 tablespoons fresh parsley, snipped
1 (20 oz.) canned tomatoes
1 (8 oz.) can tomato sauce
1/4 lb. lasagna noodles (4 noodles)
1/4 lb. natural Swiss cheese, thinly sliced
1 1/2 cups low fat cottage cheese
2 tablespoons fresh parsley, snipped

PREPARATION

Sauté onion in oil until tender. Add beef and cook until no longer pink. Slice garlic, mash with salt; add to meat, along with pepper, oregano, parsley, tomatoes and tomato sauce. Simmer, uncovered, 30 minutes.

Cook noodles according to package directions; drain and cover with cold water.

In baking dish, spread 1/3 meat sauce, top with 2 noodles, 1/2 Swiss cheese (reserving 1 slice), 1/2 cottage cheese. Repeat, ending with sauce and 1 slice Swiss cheese, slivered. Bake 30 minutes at 350 degrees F. Top with 2 tablespoons parsley.

Lasagna

4 to 6 servings

INGREDIENTS

1 (8 oz.) pkg. lasagna noodles
1 lb. lean hamburger
6 oz. ground pork
3/4 cup onion, chopped
1 clove garlic, chopped
1 (1 lb.) can tomatoes, or frozen or fresh
1 (15 oz.) can tomato sauce
1 teaspoon salt
1 teaspoon basil leaves
2 tablespoons parsley flakes
2 tablespoons granulated sugar

Cheese Mixture:
1 (24 oz.) carton cottage cheese, reduced fat
1/2 cup Parmesan cheese
1 tablespoon parsley flakes
1 1/2 teaspoon salt
1 teaspoon oregano
3/4 lb. reduced fat shredded mozzarella cheese
1/2 cup Parmesan cheese

PREPARATION

Cook noodles according to package directions; drain and set aside.

Cook hamburger and ground pork, onion and garlic in large saucepan until onion is tender; drain fat. Add tomatoes and tomato sauce, 1 teaspoon salt and basil, 2 tablespoons parsley flakes and sugar. Bring to boiling, stirring occasionally. Lower heat and simmer 1 hour, or until mixture is thickens.

Mix cottage cheese, 1/2 cup Parmesan cheese, 1 tablespoon parsley flakes, 1 1/2 teaspoons salt and oregano.

Reserve 1/2 cup sauce for top layer. In an ungreased 9x13-inch baking dish, layer 1/4 each of noodles, meat sauce, mozzarella cheese and cheese mixture. Repeat 3 times. Spread with reserved sauce.

Bake at 350 degrees F. for 45 minutes.

Easy-Does-It Pizza Casserole

6 servings

INGREDIENTS

1 lb. ground pork
1/2 cup onion, chopped
1 1/2 cups elbow macaroni
1 (8 oz.) can tomato sauce
1 (8 oz.) carton low fat cottage cheese
4 oz. (1 cup) reduced fat mozzarella cheese, shredded
1 (4 oz.) pkg. sliced pepperoni or Canadian bacon, cut in pieces (Optional)
1 teaspoon basil leaves
1/2 teaspoon oregano leaves
1 tablespoon Parmesan cheese

PREPARATION

Cook macaroni according to package directions; drain.

Brown ground pork and onion until meat is no longer pink; drain. In a 2-quart casserole dish, combine all ingredients except Parmesan cheese. Top with Parmesan cheese. Cover and bake at 350 degrees for 30 to 35 minutes or until heated.

Chicken and Pasta Primavera

6 servings

INGREDIENTS

1 (16 oz.) pkg. vermicelli
3 tablespoons butter
1/4 cup grated Parmesan cheese
1/4 cup olive oil
1 clove garlic, minced
2 boneless, skinless chicken breasts, cut in thin strips
3/4 cup tomato sauce
3/4 cup chicken broth*
Salt and pepper to taste
2 cups broccoli florets
1 cup sliced zucchini
2 carrots, sliced
1 red bell pepper, seeded and sliced

PREPARATION

Cook pasta according to package directions; drain. Toss with butter and Parmesan cheese. Keep warm. While vermicelli is cooking, heat olive oil in a saucepan. Add garlic and chicken; sauté until browned. Add all remaining ingredients, mixing well. Simmer for 10 minutes, stirring occasionally. Place vermicelli in heated serving bowl. Spoon chicken mixture on top and serve at once. *Chicken stock/broth recipe page 164.*

French Beef Au Gratin with Fettucine

4 servings

INGREDIENTS

2 cups fettuccine
1/2 cup butter
4 cups onions, thinly sliced
1 lb. sirloin or beef tenderloin, cut into 1/2 inch cubes
3 tablespoons flour
1 tablespoon dark brown sugar, packed
1 teaspoon cumin
1 teaspoon salt
1/2 teaspoon black pepper
1 quart beef broth*
1 cup (4 oz.) reduced fat mozzarella cheese, shredded
1/2 cup Parmesan cheese

PREPARATION

Cook the fettuccine according to directions on package; drain.

In a large, heavy-bottomed skillet, melt butter. Add onions and sauté until caramelized, 15 to 20 minutes. Using a slotted spoon, place onions in a medium bowl. Add beef to skillet and brown all sides. Return onions and juices to skillet.

Mix flour, brown sugar, cumin, salt and pepper in a small bowl. Add to beef mixture and heat until bubbling, about 1 minute. Gradually add beef broth; simmer 10 minutes, stirring occasionally.

Divide fettuccine into 4 ovenproof bowls and spoon beef mixture over pasta. Mix Parmesan and mozzarella cheese together; sprinkle evenly over beef. Broil about 5 minutes, until cheese is melted and lightly browned.

Beef stock/broth recipe page 162

Rigatoni

8 servings

INGREDIENTS

8 oz. rigatoni
1/4 cup olive oil
1 lb. lean ground beef
1/2 cup onion, chopped
2 (6 oz. each) cans tomato paste
2 cups water
1 1/2 teaspoon salt
2 tablespoons dried parsley
4 teaspoon dried basil
1 large clove garlic, minced
1/8 teaspoon black pepper
1 teaspoon anise seeds

Filling:

1 1/2 cups low fat small-curd cottage cheese
1 egg, beaten
1/4 teaspoon salt
1/2 cup Parmesan cheese
2 tablespoons parsley

PREPARATION

Cook the rigatoni according to package directions; drain.

Sauce:
Brown ground beef and onions in olive oil. Add tomato paste, water, salt, parsley, basil, garlic clove, pepper and anise seeds; simmer, uncovered, for 45 minutes, stirring occasionally.

Filling:
In a medium bowl, combine cottage cheese, egg, salt, Parmesan cheese and parsley.

Pour 1/3 of the meat sauce into a 2-quart baking dish. Layer 1/2 the noodles, 1/2 the cheese filling, 1/3 meat sauce, remaining halves of the noodles, cheese and remaining meat sauce. Sprinkle with Parmesan cheese.

Bake at 350 degrees F. for 25 to 30 minutes.

Pork Medallions with Apple-Yogurt Sauce

4 servings

INGREDIENTS

2 cups fettuccine
3/4 lb. pork tenderloin
1/2 cup unsweetened apple juice
1 cup thinly sliced apple
1/3 cup chopped onion
1/4 teaspoon dried sage, crushed
1/4 teaspoon salt
1 (8 oz.) container plain low-fat yogurt
2 tablespoons flour
Snipped chives (optional)
Sage sprigs (optional)
1 tiny red onion, cut in half (optional)
Non-stick cooking spray

PREPARATION

Cook noodles according to package directions; drain.

Trim fat from pork and cut in1-inch thick slices. Place portions between sheets of plastic wrap and pound to 1/2-inch. Spray a skillet with non-stick cooking spray; preheat to medium hot. Add meat to skillet; cook for 3 minutes. Turn and cook meat an additional 3 to 4 minutes, until no pink remains. Remove meat; set aside.

To the skillet, add apple juice, apple slices, onion, dried sage and salt to skillet. Cook, covered for 5 minutes or until onion is tender. Combine yogurt and flour; add yogurt mixture to skillet. Cook, stirring constantly, until mixture thickens. Cook and stir for 1 minute more.

Arrange pork on top of fettuccine. Spoon sauce over pork. If desired, sprinkle with chives and garnish with fresh sage and red onion halves.

Easy Baked Spaghetti

4 servings

INGREDIENTS

2 slices bacon, diced
1 clove garlic, minced
2 medium onions, chopped
1/2 lb. lean ground beef
2 1/2 cups water
2 (8 oz. each) cans tomato sauce
1 1/2 teaspoons salt
Black pepper to taste
1 teaspoon chili powder
1/2 cup black olives, sliced
8 oz. spaghetti
1 1/2 cups cheddar cheese, shredded
Non-stick cooking spray

PREPARATION

In a large skillet, fry bacon until crispy; add garlic and onions; cook until soft. Add ground beef; cook until brown. Stir in water, tomato sauce, salt, pepper and chili powder. Simmer covered 25 minutes. Stir in black olives.

Break spaghetti in half and put in a 2-quart casserole dish sprayed with non-stick cooking spray. Cover with half of tomato sauce mixture. Sprinkle with half of cheese. Repeat layers. Cover and bake at 350 degrees F. for 30 minutes. Uncover, bake 15 minutes longer.

Italian Vegetable Chicken and Pasta

4 servings

INGREDIENTS

1/2 lb. linguine or vermicelli
1 cup zucchini halved, sliced
1 1/4 cups yellow squash, quartered, sliced
2 tablespoons olive oil
1/2 cup asparagus, cut into 1" pieces
2 cloves garlic, diced
1/3 cup red bell pepper, julienned
2 green onions, sliced
1/2 cup mushrooms, sliced
3 Roma tomatoes, diced
3 chicken breasts, cooked, diced
2 cups whipping cream or half and half
1 teaspoon white pepper
1/2 cup Parmesan cheese, freshly shredded

PREPARATION

Cook pasta according to package directions; drain and set aside.

In a large skillet, sauté zucchini and yellow squash in olive oil for 1 minute. Add asparagus, garlic, bell pepper, green onions and mushrooms. Sauté 3 to 4 minutes until vegetables start to soften.

Add tomatoes and chicken; cook 1 to 2 minutes. Add cooked pasta to heat. In a separate medium saucepan, heat cream until bubbly. Continue to cook about 4 to 5 minutes until it starts to reduce. Add white pepper. Pour cream over vegetables and chicken; add cheese and toss. Serve immediately.

Chicken Risotto with Orzo

4 servings

INGREDIENTS

4 cups chicken broth*
1 3/4 to 2 cups water
1 medium zucchini, 1/2-inch dice
1 medium onion, 1/2-inch dice
1 tablespoon olive oil, divided
4 chicken breasts (1 1/2 lb., whole or diced)
1 garlic clove, pressed
1/4 teaspoon salt
2 cups orzo
1/4 cup carrots, diced
1/4 teaspoon thyme
1/2 cup grated Parmesan cheese pepper

PREPARATION

In a large saucepan, simmer chicken broth and water.

Coat zucchini and onion with 1-1/2 teaspoons olive oil; spread on baking sheet and bake at 450 degrees F. for 6 minutes or until edges of vegetables brown. Remove from oven and set aside.

Heat the remaining 1-1/2 teaspoons olive oil on high heat; sauté chicken and garlic until done. Salt chicken.

Move chicken to edge and toast orzo until golden (2 minutes).

Reduce heat and add carrots; stir in hot broth mixture 1 cup at a time as orzo absorbs liquid, about 10 minutes. Reserve 1/4 cup of broth. Stir in roasted vegetables, cheese and the reserved 1/4 cup of broth. Serve immediately.

Chicken stock/broth recipe page 164

Chicken Gorgonzola

4 servings

INGREDIENTS

6 oz. fresh ziti or penne pasta
6 to 7 oz. boneless, skinless chicken breast
1/2 cup flour for coating
1/8 teaspoon black pepper
1/4 teaspoon salt
2 tablespoons olive oil
2 teaspoons fresh shallots, minced
2 teaspoons fresh garlic, minced
2 tablespoon pine nuts
1/2 cup chicken broth
2 oz. heavy cream
1 cup tomatoes, diced
2 tablespoons fresh basil, minced
2 cups fresh spinach, julienned, lightly packed
1/8 teaspoon Italian seasoning
1 1/2 cups Gorgonzola cheese, grated

PREPARATION

Cook pasta according to package directions; drain.

Trim chicken, cutting off any fat or cartilage; Cut into half-inch strips. Blend flour with salt and pepper; dredge chicken in flour and shake off excess. Sauté both sides of chicken in olive oil until brown, about 3 minutes. Add shallots, garlic and pine nuts; simmer 2 to 3 minutes on low heat.

Add chicken broth and bring to boil; reduce liquid by half. Add cream, tomatoes, basil, spinach and Italian seasoning. Add hot drained pasta, Gorgonzola and stir.

Mediterranean Chicken with Feta Cheese and Tomatoes

4 servings

INGREDIENTS

12 Kalamata olives, chopped
10 oz. grape tomatoes, quartered
1/4 cup capers, rinsed and drained
1/4 cup snipped fresh parsley
2 teaspoons olive oil
2 tablespoons red wine vinegar
1 1/2 teaspoons crumbled dried basil
1 lb. boneless, skinless chicken pieces
1 (14.5 oz.) can fat-free chicken broth*
1 cup orzo
2 oz. feta cheese with sun-dried tomatoes
Non-stick cooking spray

PREPARATION

In a large bowl, combine olives, tomatoes, capers, parsley, olive oil, vinegar and 1 teaspoon basil. Set aside.

Spray a large non-stick skillet with non-stick cooking spray and heat. Cook chicken smooth side down for 20 minutes on medium-high heat. Remove chicken to a platter.

Add the chicken broth and orzo to the chicken drippings in the skillet; bring to a boil, scraping up browned bits. In the skillet, arrange chicken, browned side up, on orzo and sprinkle with 1/2 teaspoon basil. Simmer, covered, for 12 minutes. Spoon cooked orzo onto individual plates and top with chicken, tomato mixture and feta cheese.

Chicken stock/broth recipe page 164

Penne Pasta Romano with Crusted Chicken & Creamy Pesto Sauce

4 servings

INGREDIENTS

8 oz. penne pasta
6 oz. boneless, skinless chicken breasts
2 oz. Italian bread crumbs
1 oz. Romano cheese
Olive oil
1/2 cup chicken broth
2 teaspoons basil pesto
Salt and pepper to taste
2 oz. butter
3 oz. heavy cream
1/2 teaspoon crushed garlic

PREPARATION

Cook pasta according to package directions; drain.

Mix bread crumbs with cheese in 2 to 1 ratio. Pound chicken, rinse with water and dredge in breading. Sauté chicken in oil until done or until chicken is no longer pink inside; set aside.

In the same pan, add chicken broth, pesto, salt and pepper. Bring to boil; reduce heat, add butter and simmer. Add cream and garlic; simmer until sauce thickens. Add pasta and sautéed chicken. Remove from heat.

Baked Turkey Tetrazzini

4 to 6 servings

INGREDIENTS

8 oz. linguine
1 tablespoon olive oil
1 white onion, chopped
1 cup fresh mushrooms, sliced
1 red bell pepper, chopped
1/3 cup flour
3 cups 2% milk
1/4 teaspoon salt
4 or 5 drops hot pepper sauce
1/4 cup fresh parsley, chopped
2 cups cooked turkey, cubed
12 sliced Kalamata olives
1/2 cup grated Parmesan cheese
1/4 cup seasoned bread crumbs
Non-stick cooking spray

PREPARATION

Cook pasta according to package directions; drain. Add a little olive oil and mix to keep it from sticking to itself.

Heat olive oil in a large skillet on medium-high heat. Add onion, mushrooms and bell pepper. Cook for 5 minutes.

In a bowl, whisk flour and milk together. Add to skillet with salt and hot pepper sauce, stirring constantly until slightly thickened, about 5 minutes.

Remove skillet from heat and add parsley, turkey, olives and Parmesan cheese. Mix well. Add linguine and toss until well mixed.

Spray a 9x13-inch baking dish with non-stick cooking spray (or two 8x8-inch baking dishes). Pour mixture into baking dish.

Top with seasoned bread crumbs and bake, covered, at 350 degrees F. for 20 minutes. Uncover and bake 10 to 15 minutes more or until it bubbles.

Chicken Tetrazzini

4 servings

INGREDIENTS

8 oz. thin spaghetti
3 tablespoons butter
3 tablespoons flour
1/4 teaspoon black pepper
1 teaspoon salt
2 cups chicken broth*
3/4 cup half and half
2 cups cooked, diced chicken
1 cup Parmesan cheese, divided
1 tablespoon butter
1 tablespoon lemon juice
8 oz. mushrooms, sliced

PREPARATION

Cook spaghetti according to package directions; drain.

Melt 3 tablespoons butter in a saucepan. Add flour and cook for 1 minute; stir in pepper and salt. Constantly stirring, slowly stir in broth. Bring to a boil and simmer until thickened. Stir in half and half, chicken and 3/4 cup Parmesan cheese.

Melt 1 tablespoon butter and lemon juice in a skillet. Sauté mushrooms until juice cooks off, about 5 minutes. Combine pasta with cream mixture and mushrooms. Place in baking dish. Bake at 375 degrees F. for 20 minutes or until heated. Add remaining cheese on top after 15 minutes.

Chicken broth recipe page 164

Chicken-Macaroni Supreme

4 to 6 servings

INGREDIENTS

2 cups macaroni
1 lb. boneless, skinless chicken, cut into strips
2 cloves garlic, minced
4 tablespoons margarine or butter, divided
2 cups broccoli, chopped
1 medium onion, chopped
1 medium red bell pepper, julienned
1 cup carrots, sliced
1/4 teaspoon tarragon leaves
1/4 teaspoon lemon pepper
2 teaspoons chicken flavor bouillon granules
1/2 cup frozen peas, thawed
1 cup low fat milk
1 tablespoon flour
1 1/2 cups American cheese, shredded

PREPARATION

Cook pasta according to directions on package; drain.

In a medium skillet, sauté chicken and garlic in 2 tablespoons butter. Cook until chicken is browned.

Remove chicken from skillet; add remaining butter, broccoli, onion, bell pepper, carrots, tarragon leaves, lemon pepper and bouillon granules to skillet. Stir-fry for 1 minute on medium-high heat. Lower heat, cover and simmer until broccoli is tender.

Add macaroni, peas and chicken to skillet; heat through. In a small bowl, blend flour with milk; add to macaroni. Add cheese and stir until melted.

Chicken Lasagna

8 to 10 servings

INGREDIENTS

8 oz. lasagna noodles
1/2 cup onion, chopped
1/2 cup green bell pepper, chopped
3 tablespoons margarine or butter
1 (10.5 oz.) can low fat cream of chicken soup*
6 oz. mushrooms, drained and sliced
1/2 cup pimento, chopped
1/2 cup low fat milk (more if needed)
1/2 teaspoon basil
1 1/2 cups low fat cottage cheese or 8 oz. reduced fat cream cheese
2 cups chicken, cooked and diced
2 cups American cheese, shredded
1/2 cup Parmesan cheese
1/4 teaspoon paprika

PREPARATION

Cook noodles according to package directions; drain.

Sauté onion and bell pepper in margarine until tender. In a large bowl, combine chicken or mushroom soup, mushrooms, pimento, milk, basil, cottage cheese or cream cheese, chicken and American cheese.

Layer noodles and mixture in 9x13-inch baking dish; top with Parmesan cheese and paprika. Bake at 350 degrees F. for 45 minutes.

Cream of chicken recipe page 166

Low-Fat Fettuccine with Chicken

2 servings

INGREDIENTS

1 tablespoon olive oil
1 boneless, skinless chicken breast, cut bite-size
1 carrot, thinly sliced
1 zucchini, thinly sliced
Salt and pepper to taste
3 tablespoons flour
2 cups chicken stock, heated*
1/4 cup whipping cream
1 cup Parmesan cheese
8 oz. fettuccine

PREPARATION

Cook noodles according to package directions; drain. Heat oil in a large skillet over medium heat. Add chicken; cook for 2 minutes. Add carrots; cook 2 minutes more. Add zucchini; season with salt and pepper and cook 2 minutes. Blend in flour.

Cover and cook 3 to 4 minutes over low heat. Pour in chicken stock; season. Stir in whipping cream. Cook 2 to 3 minutes, uncovered, over medium heat. Stir in Parmesan cheese; cook 2 more minutes. Add pasta; cook 1 minute to reheat. *Chicken stock recipe pg. 164*

Chicken, Macaroni, Vegetable Casserole

3 to 4 servings

INGREDIENTS

1 cup elbow macaroni, uncooked
1 1/2 cups cooked chicken, diced
2 oz. Swiss cheese
2 oz. American cheese
1 small onion, chopped
Salt and pepper, to taste
1 (10.5 oz.) can low fat cream of mushroom soup*
3/4 cup low-fat chicken broth**
1 cup low fat milk
Peas or chopped broccoli, to taste
Non-stick cooking spray
1/2 cup corn flakes, crushed

PREPARATION

In a large bowl, combine all ingredients. Pour into an 8x8-inch baking dish sprayed with non-stick cooking spray. Seal and refrigerate 6 hours or overnight.

Bake, uncovered at 350 degrees F. for 45 minutes. Combine crushed corn flakes and 1/2 tablespoon butter. Add corn flake mixture as topping to casserole.
*Cream of mushroom pg. 161   **Chicken broth pg. 164*

Chicken and Peppers over Pasta

6 servings

INGREDIENTS

8 large red bell peppers, roasted
1 large onion, chopped
5 tablespoons olive oil, divided
2 garlic cloves, pressed
1/2 teaspoon salt
1/4 teaspoon black pepper
1/2 teaspoon granulated sugar
1 teaspoon oregano
1 (28 oz.) can whole tomatoes
2 lb. boneless, skinless chicken breasts
1/2 cup white wine
1 (16 oz.) pkg. spaghetti
1/4 cup butter, melted
1/4 cup grated Parmesan cheese

PREPARATION

Roast red peppers on the stove or grill until blackened. Peel, remove the seeds and cut roasted peppers into 1-inch pieces.

Sauté onion in 3 tablespoons of olive oil in a large skillet until the onion is translucent. Add garlic, roasted peppers, salt, black pepper, sugar and oregano. Slice the canned tomatoes and add to onion mixture, along with the liquid from the can.

Cut the chicken breasts into 3/4-inch cubes and brown lightly in a separate skillet in a small amount of olive oil. Add chicken to the onion mixture.

Deglaze the chicken skillet with the white wine. Add the wine mixture to the chicken mixture. Simmer, covered, for 45 minutes to 1 hour or until the chicken is cooked through and tender.

Cook spaghetti according to package directions; drain. Place the pasta in a large warm bowl. Add the melted butter and Parmesan cheese; toss to combine. Serve the chicken mixture over the prepared pasta.

White Spaghetti

8 to 10 servings

INGREDIENTS

8 oz. spaghetti
1/4 cup butter or margarine
1/3 cup flour
1/4 teaspoon garlic powder
1 tablespoon onion, minced
1/8 teaspoon black pepper
1 cup milk
2 cups chicken broth*
1 cup Romano or Parmesan cheese, divided
1 (4 oz.) can sliced mushrooms, drained
3/4 lb. fresh asparagus or 1 (10 oz.) pkg. frozen
asparagus, cooked and drained
2 cups cooked chicken, cubed
12 oz. reduced fat mozzarella cheese, shredded or
sliced
6 oz. sliced ham, thinly chopped
Non-stick cooking spray

PREPARATION

Cook spaghetti according to package directions; drain.

In a large saucepan, melt butter or margarine. Stir in
flour, garlic powder, onion and black pepper. Mix in

milk and chicken broth; cook, stirring constantly, until thickened. Blend in 1/2 cup Romano cheese. Remove from heat and add mushrooms.

Spray a 13x9-inch baking dish with non-stick cooking spray. Layer 1/2 cup chicken broth mixture in baking dish.

Spread one-third of the cooked spaghetti in baking dish over chicken broth mixture. Top with asparagus, chicken, mozzarella and about 1 cup chicken broth mixture. Add a layer of ham, one-third of the cooked spaghetti and half of the remaining chicken broth mixture.

Cover with remaining spaghetti and chicken broth mixture. Sprinkle with remaining Romano cheese. Bake at 350 degrees F. for 35 minutes, uncovered.

Chicken stock/broth recipe page 164

Dutch Oven Chicken

4 to 6 servings

INGREDIENTS

1 medium onion, chopped
1/2 cup celery, chopped
3 tablespoons margarine
2 cups cooked chicken, cubed
6 oz. uncooked spaghetti (broken into pieces)
1 (10.5 oz.) can reduced fat cream of celery soup
2 cups chicken broth*
1 teaspoon lemon juice
1/4 teaspoon black pepper
1/8 teaspoon nutmeg

PREPARATION

Sauté onion and celery with margarine in a Dutch oven; add chicken and spaghetti to the onion mixture.

In a large bowl, combine soup, broth, lemon juice, pepper, nutmeg and pour evenly over the entire surface. Cover and bring to a boil. Reduce heat and simmer for 20 minutes, stirring once.

Chicken stock/broth recipe page 164

Stuffed Jumbo Shells

4 servings

INGREDIENTS

24 jumbo pasta shells
8 oz. low fat Ricotta cheese
8 oz. low fat cottage cheese
16 oz. reduced fat mozzarella, shredded
1 tablespoon parsley flakes
1 teaspoon salt
1/4 teaspoon black pepper
1/2 lb. Italian sausage or lean ground beef
1 (32 oz.) jar spaghetti sauce
1/4 cup additional mozzarella cheese

PREPARATION

Cook shells according to package directions; drain.

In a medium bowl, mix Ricotta, cottage cheese, mozzarella, parsley, salt and pepper. Stuff each shell with cheese mixture. Place in 9x13-inch baking dish.

Cook meat; drain. Combine spaghetti sauce and meat. Pour over shells. Sprinkle mozzarella on top (1/4 cup). Bake at 350 degrees F. for 30 minutes.

Seafood Pastas

Stir-Fried Shrimp with Angel Hair Pasta

8 servings

INGREDIENTS

1 (16 oz.) pkg. angel hair pasta
1 cup chicken broth*
5 tablespoons rice vinegar
1 tablespoon soy sauce
1 tablespoon cornstarch
1 teaspoon granulated sugar
1 tablespoon light sesame or olive oil
1 1/2 lb. shelled deveined uncooked medium shrimp
1/4 cup chopped green onions
2 tablespoons grated ginger root
5 garlic cloves, minced
1 (15 oz.) can baby corn, drained
1 (9 oz.) pkg. frozen sugar snap peas, thawed, drained

PREPARATION

Cook pasta according to package directions; drain and cover to keep warm.

Mix broth, vinegar, soy sauce, cornstarch and sugar; blend well and set aside.

In a large skillet, sauté shrimp, onions, ginger root and garlic in oil, stirring until shrimp turn pink. Stir in broth mixture, corn and sugar snap peas; cook and stir 2 to 4 minutes or until sauce thickens slightly. Serve shrimp mixture over pasta.

Chicken stock/broth recipe page 164

Pasta with Asparagus and Shrimp

4 servings

INGREDIENTS

12 oz. linguine
24 asparagus spears
1/2 lb. shrimp
1 teaspoon grated lemon zest
2 1/2 tablespoons fresh lemon juice
2 cloves garlic, minced
2 tablespoons fresh parsley
Black pepper to taste
1/4 teaspoon salt
2 teaspoons Dijon mustard
1/3 cup + 3 tablespoons olive or saffron oil, divided
1 large red bell pepper or roasted peppers
1 cup black olives, halved

PREPARATION

Cook pasta according to package directions; drain and coat with 3 tablespoons olive oil.

Steam asparagus; reserve 3 tablespoons of the water. Use remaining asparagus water to steam shrimp 3 to 5 minutes.

Whisk reserved 3 tablespoons water, lemon zest, lemon juice, garlic, parsley, pepper, salt and mustard with 1/3 cup olive oil or saffron oil. Toss together linguine, shrimp, asparagus, peppers and olives with lemon juice mixture. Cool before serving.

Elegant Spaghetti with Shrimp

4 to 6 servings

INGREDIENTS

1/2 cup olive oil
5 cloves garlic, minced
1 teaspoon oregano
1/2 cup white wine
6 to 8 oz. frozen shrimp, deveined
8 oz. spaghetti
Salt and pepper
Parmesan or Romano cheese, grated

PREPARATION

In a medium saucepan, slowly heat the olive oil on medium heat. Add garlic and oregano; sauté until garlic begins to brown. Remove from heat; cool. Remove the garlic and discard. Add wine to oil and heat until bubbling. Add shrimp and cook. Shrimp should be thawed and patted dry on paper towels.

Bring 4 quarts salted water to a boil in large pot. Stirring constantly, gradually add spaghetti to boiling water. When spaghetti and water reach a full boil, cover and turn off heat. Let it stand exactly 10 minutes, stirring several times.

Pour spaghetti into large colander and drain; do not rinse. Shake and pour spaghetti back into hot pot. Pour hot oil, wine and shrimp sauce over spaghetti and toss. Add salt, pepper and cheese as desired.

Scallops and Shrimp with Linguine

6 servings

INGREDIENTS

1 (10 oz.) pkg. linguine
1 lb. scallops
1/2 lb. shrimp
1/2 cup green onion, sliced
3 cloves garlic, finely diced
3 tablespoons olive oil
3 tablespoons margarine or butter
1 teaspoon basil
2 teaspoons parsley
Crushed red pepper to taste
2 cups fresh pea pods
1 small tomato, diced and seeds
3 tablespoons fresh Romano cheese

PREPARATION

Cook pasta according to package directions; drain.

If seafood is frozen, thaw. Halve scallops. Remove veins and peel shrimp. Mix scallops and shrimp in bowl.

In a large skillet over medium high heat, sauté onion and garlic in olive oil and margarine or butter for 30 seconds. Add 1/2 scallops and shrimp, basil, parsley and red pepper. Stirring often, sauté until shrimp turns pink and scallops are no longer translucent. Leaving the oil in the skillet, scoop out mixture. Cook remaining seafood. Place all seafood mixture in the skillet.

Cut peas pods in half and add with tomatoes to seafood. Cook to heat vegetables. Toss linguine with seafood mixture in a large bowl. Serve with fresh Romano cheese and extra crushed red pepper.

Grilled Tuna Pasta Toss

4 servings

INGREDIENTS

8 oz. angel hair pasta
1 lb. fresh tuna steak
1 teaspoon dried basil, divided
1 teaspoon seasoning salt, divided
2 tablespoons olive oil
1 teaspoon garlic, minced
1/2 large white onion, chopped
5 oz. fresh spinach (about 3 handfuls of fresh spinach)
1/4 cup sun-dried tomatoes, diced (optional)
2 tablespoons capers

PREPARATION

Cook pasta according to package directions; drain.

Season tuna steak with 1/2 teaspoon basil and 1/2 teaspoon seasoning salt. Grill or broil, being careful not to overcook. After cooking, cool, then flake into small pieces; set aside.

In a large skillet, heat olive oil and sauté garlic with remaining 1/2 teaspoon seasoning salt. When garlic just starts to brown, add onion, remaining 1/2 teaspoon basil, spinach and sun-dried tomatoes (if using).

Continue cooking until onion and spinach are done, 3 to 5 minutes on medium-high heat. Lower heat; add cooked and drained pasta, tuna and capers; toss well.

Baked Tuna and Cheese Casserole

6 servings

INGREDIENTS

1 cup elbow macaroni
5 tablespoons butter or margarine
1/4 cup onion, chopped
1/4 cup flour
1/8 teaspoon black pepper
1 1/2 teaspoons salt
2 1/2 cups milk
1 cup cheese (cheddar or American), shredded
1 (12 oz.) can white chunk tuna
Optional: 1/4 cup sliced olives, diced carrots

PREPARATION

Cook pasta according to directions on package; drain.

Melt butter in saucepan and sauté onion until golden. Remove from heat and add flour, pepper salt; stir until smooth. Stir in milk gradually. Continuing to stir, bring milk mixture to boil for 1 minute. Lower heat and add cheese. (You can add more cheese for a richer sauce). Stir over low heat until smooth. Combine macaroni, vegetables and cheese sauce together. Mix in tuna and place in buttered casserole dish. Bake at 350 degrees F. for 20 to 30 minutes.

Orzo Shrimp Stew

4 servings

INGREDIENTS

2 1/2 cups chicken broth*
1 (14.5 oz.) can Italian style tomatoes, diced (reserve liquid)
5 cups broccoli, coarsely chopped
1 cup orzo
1 lb. raw shrimp, medium
2 tablespoons margarine or butter
Salt and pepper to taste

PREPARATION

In a large saucepan, heat broth to boil. Add tomatoes, broccoli and orzo. When broth returns to boil, stir in shrimp. Simmer until shrimp becomes opaque and pasta is cooked. Stir in margarine or butter. Season with salt and pepper.

Chicken stock/broth recipe page 164

Crab and Spaghetti Bake

6 servings

INGREDIENTS

6 oz. spaghetti or vermicelli
1 large onion, chopped
2 tablespoons butter or margarine
1 (10.5 oz.) can low fat cream of mushroom soup*
1 cup half-and-half
1 tablespoon Worcestershire sauce
1 tablespoon Dijon mustard
1/2 lb. cooked fresh or canned crab
2 hard-cooked eggs, diced
1/2 cup sliced water chestnuts
1 jar (2 oz.) sliced pimentos, drained
Salt and cayenne pepper to taste
2/3 cup shredded sharp Cheddar cheese
Non-stick cooking spray

PREPARATION

Cook pasta according to package directions; drain.

In a large skillet, sauté onion in butter or margarine until soft. Blend in soup, half-and-half, Worcestershire sauce and mustard. Add spaghetti, crab, eggs, water chestnuts, and pimentos; toss gently. Season to taste with salt and red pepper.

Spoon spaghetti mixture into a shallow 2-quart casserole dish or 9-inch square baking dish, lightly sprayed with non-stick cooking spray. Sprinkle with cheese.

Bake uncovered at 375 degrees for about 25 minutes or until bubbly and heated through.

Cream of mushroom soup recipe page 161

Farfalle with Salmon Sauce

4 to 6 servings

INGREDIENTS

12 oz. farfalle
1 1/2 to 2 tablespoons lemon juice
2 tablespoons dry white wine
1 cup heavy whipping cream
Salt and pepper to taste
3 tablespoons finely chopped fresh dill
1/4 lb. smoked salmon, cut into thin strips

PREPARATION

Cook pasta according to package directions; drain and set aside.

Cook lemon juice and wine to reduce; lower heat and add cream. Cook, stirring constantly, until sauce thickens, about 10 minutes. Add salt, pepper, dill and salmon; heat. Ladle sauce over pasta and serve.

Vermicelli with Fresh Clams

6 to 8 servings

INGREDIENTS

1 (16 oz.) pkg. vermicelli
2 lb. clams in their shells
2 cloves garlic, peeled
1/2 cup olive oil
1/4 cup chopped parsley
Salt and pepper to taste
1/4 cup butter, melted

PREPARATION

Cook pasta according to package directions; drain and place in heated serving dish.

Scrub clams and soak in cold water for 1 hour; drain. In large, heavy skillet, sauté garlic in olive oil until browned; remove garlic from skillet and discard. Add clams, cover, and cook over medium heat for 5 minutes. Add parsley, salt and pepper; cook 3 minutes more.

Remove clams from skillet. Strain skillet liquid through cheesecloth to remove any grit. Toss vermicelli with skillet liquid. Place clams on top, drizzle with melted butter and serve immediately.

Green Fettuccine with Scallop and Parsley Sauce

10 servings

INGREDIENTS

1/4 cup fresh parsley, minced
1 shallot, minced
4 tablespoons butter
1/2 cup dry white wine
1 pound sea scallops, cut horizontally into 1 inch slices
1 cup low fat evaporated milk
1/2 cup heavy cream
1 cup Parmesan cheese, plus additional for serving
1/3 cup plus 2 tablespoons fresh parsley, minced
Freshly grated nutmeg
Salt and pepper to taste
1 1/2 lb. green fettuccine
2 tablespoons unsalted butter, softened

PREPARATION

Over medium heat and using a stainless-steel or enameled skillet, cook 1/4 cup parsley and shallots in butter for 5 minutes. Add wine and reduce over high heat until about 6 tablespoons of liquid remain.

Add the scallops and cook for 1 minute. Add both evaporated milk and heavy cream; simmer for 2 minutes. Remove from heat and add 1 cup Parmesan cheese, 1/3 cup minced parsley and nutmeg. Salt and pepper to taste.

Cook noodles according to package directions; drain and toss with unsalted butter. Transfer the pasta to a heated serving dish and ladle on the sauce. Toss gently and sprinkle with 2 tablespoons of minced parsley and Parmesan cheese.

Catfish with Lemon and Butter Sauce

6 to 8 servings

INGREDIENTS

1 (16 oz.) pkg. spaghetti
3/4 cup butter
1 garlic clove, minced
8 oz. fresh mushrooms, sliced
1 teaspoon salt
1/2 teaspoon black pepper
1/2 cup chicken broth
2 teaspoons lemon juice
1/4 cup fresh parsley, chopped
1 1/2 lb. catfish fillets, cut into 1 inch pieces
1/2 cup Parmesan cheese

PREPARATION

Cook spaghetti according to package directions; drain.

In a large skillet, melt butter over medium heat. Cook garlic and mushrooms for 5 minutes. Add salt, pepper, broth, lemon juice and parsley. Cook 3 minutes, stirring occasionally. Leave skillet uncovered, add catfish and simmer until fish flakes easily with fork, about 6 to 8 minutes. Sauce will be thin. Serve over spaghetti and sprinkle with Parmesan cheese.

 # Veggie Pastas

Angel Hair Pasta with Chickpeas

4 servings

INGREDIENTS

1/2 cup olive oil
1/3 cup white wine vinegar
1/2 teaspoon salt
1/4 teaspoon black pepper
3 tablespoons coarsely chopped fresh basil, or 1 1/2 teaspoons dried
2 teaspoons capers, drained
1/2 lb. angel hair pasta
1 (8 oz.) can garbanzos chick peas

PREPARATION

Dressing: Whisk olive oil, vinegar, salt, and pepper together. Stir in basil and drained capers; set aside. Cook pasta according to package directions; drain. Place chickpeas in strainer and rinse under cold running water; drain. Add chickpeas and vinaigrette to pasta and toss to combine.

Pasta Primavera

4 servings

INGREDIENTS

8 oz. spaghetti or angel hair pasta
8 oz. fresh asparagus
4 oz. fresh snow peas
2 tablespoons olive oil
1/2 cup onion, minced
1 yellow squash, sliced thin
2 plum tomatoes, diced
1 cup cream
1/2 teaspoon salt
1/4 teaspoon black pepper
1/2 cup Parmesan cheese

PREPARATION

Cook spaghetti according to package directions; drain.

Cut asparagus into 1/2-inch pieces; cook in a saucepan of boiling water for 1 minute. Remove. Add snow peas to boiling water and cook 30 seconds. Rinse peas and asparagus in cold water; drain.

In a large skillet, heat olive oil over medium heat. Add onion and yellow squash; cook 2 minutes. Add asparagus, snow peas and tomatoes; cook 2 minutes.

Add cream and bring to boil. Reduce heat and simmer for 2 minutes. Season with salt and pepper. Toss with cooked spaghetti or angel hair pasta and garnish with Parmesan cheese.

Brunch Frittata

8 servings

INGREDIENTS

8 oz. vermicelli
3/4 cup (3 oz.) Swiss cheese, shredded
1/2 cup green bell pepper, chopped
1 medium tomato, chopped
1/2 cup sliced ripe olives
4 eggs, beaten, or 1 (8 oz.) carton egg substitute
1/4 cup low fat milk
1/2 cup Parmesan cheese, freshly grated
Salt and pepper to taste
1 (26 oz.) jar roasted peppers and onion pasta sauce, heated
Non-stick cooking spray

PREPARATION

Cook pasta according to package directions; drain.

Spray a 9-inch springform or 9-inch round cake pan with non-stick cooking spray. Spread pasta in pan. Cover with Swiss cheese, bell pepper, tomato and olives.

Mix eggs, milk, Parmesan cheese, salt and pepper. Pour mixture into pan; press with a spoon to moisten vegetables and pasta. Bake, covered, at 350 degrees F. for 25 minutes. Uncover and continue to bake 20 minutes. Serve warm topped with pasta sauce.

NOTE: Leftover pasta may be used. Cheddar, provolone or other cheese can be substituted for the Swiss. Other vegetables may be substituted, such as chopped celery onion, red bell pepper or green chilies.

Oriental Vegetable and Peanut Pasta

6 servings

INGREDIENTS

1 (16 oz.) pkg. vermicelli
1/2 cup onion, finely chopped
1 1/2 tablespoons rice vinegar
1 tablespoon dry sherry
1 tablespoon chopped fresh ginger or 1 teaspoon powder ginger
3 tablespoons plus 1 teaspoon sesame oil
1 teaspoon dry mustard
1/8 teaspoon cayenne pepper
1/2 lb. tofu
1/4 cup peanut butter
3 tablespoons tamari
1 cup snow pea pods
1 cup small broccoli florets
1/2 cup button mushrooms

PREPARATION

Cook pasta according to package directions; drain.

Puree onion, vinegar, sherry, ginger, 1 teaspoon sesame oil, mustard, cayenne pepper, tofu, peanut butter and tamari together in a food processor or blender. Place in a saucepan and heat over low heat.

Heat 3 tablespoons oil in wok or skillet; stir-fry pea pods, broccoli and mushrooms until crisp-tender. Toss pasta, puree and vegetables together.

Angel Hair Pasta with Onions and Peppers

2 to 3 servings

INGREDIENTS

1 lemon
Small red onion
1 lb. white or yellow onions
1/4 cup olive oil
3/4 teaspoon salt
1/4 teaspoon black pepper
1/8 teaspoon of granulated sugar
1 red bell pepper
2 oz. Parmesan cheese
8 oz. angel hair pasta
2 to 4 tablespoons unsalted butter
2 tablespoons chopped fresh parsley

PREPARATION

Wash lemon, dry and cut in half lengthwise. Remove peel from one half of lemon, avoiding white pith; reserve remaining half for another use.

Peel red onion; cut into thin slices, separate into rings and set aside. Peel and quarter white or yellow onions; cut into thin slivers. You will have about 1/2 cup red onion and about 2 cups white or yellow onions.

Heat olive oil in a saucepan over low heat. Add lemon peel and sauté 2 minutes. Stir in slivered onions, salt, pepper and sugar. Raise heat to medium, cover the saucepan and simmer, stirring occasionally to prevent sticking, 20 to 30 minutes, or until onions are well browned.

Wash and dry red bell pepper. Halve, core, seed pepper and cut into 1/2-inch-thick strips. Grate Parmesan cheese to measure 1/2 cup.

In a large saucepan, bring 3 quarts of water to a boil over high heat. Add pasta to boiling water and, after water returns to a boil, cook about 30 seconds. Turn pasta into colander to drain.

Add pasta to onions in saucepan and toss gently. Add red onion rings, pepper strips, butter to taste, parsley, and 1/4 cup grated Parmesan cheese to pasta, and toss. Divide pasta among bowls and serve with remaining Parmesan cheese.

Baked Tomato Pasta

4 to 6 servings

INGREDIENTS

1 lb. penne pasta
2/3 cup olive oil
1 1/2 lb. plum tomatoes, slice in half lengthwise
Salt and pepper to taste
1/4 cup dry bread crumbs, plain
1/4 cup Parmesan cheese, grated
3 cloves garlic, minced
2 teaspoons granulated sugar
1 teaspoon dried oregano or Italian seasoning

PREPARATION

Cook pasta according to package directions; drain.

Pour olive oil in a 9x13-inch baking dish. Dip cut sides of tomatoes in oil; arrange in dish cut-side up. Fit tomatoes closely together in 1 layer. Sprinkle with salt and pepper.

In a small bowl, combine bread crumbs, cheese, garlic, sugar, oregano or Italian seasoning; sprinkle over tomatoes. Bake at 375 degrees F. for 40 minutes. Toss pasta with baked tomatoes.

Spinach Lasagna

4 to 6 servings

INGREDIENTS

8 oz. (9 strips) lasagna noodles
2 lb. (or 12 oz.) low fat cottage cheese
2 eggs
1 teaspoon salt
1/4 teaspoon black pepper
1/2 teaspoon garlic powder
1/4 cup soft margarine
1 lb. Monterey Jack, grated
2 (9 oz. each) pkg. frozen spinach, cooked and drained
1 cup Parmesan cheese
1 tablespoon parsley
Non-stick cooking spray

PREPARATION

Cook noodles according to package directions; drain.

In a large bowl, mix cottage cheese, eggs, salt, pepper, garlic powder and margarine. Spray a 9x13-inch baking dish with non-stick cooking spray and place a layer of cooked noodles in the bottom, followed by cottage cheese mix, Monterey Jack, a layer of spinach and Parmesan cheese. Repeat layers. Bake, uncovered, 30 minutes at 350 degrees F.

Tofu Lasagna

6 servings

INGREDIENTS

12.3 oz. firm tofu, diced
2 cups low fat mozzarella cheese, shredded, divided
2 eggs, lightly beaten
10 oz. chopped frozen spinach, thawed and drained
2 teaspoons fresh parsley, chopped
1/2 teaspoon basil leaves
1/4 teaspoon salt
1/4 teaspoon black pepper
1/8 teaspoon ground nutmeg
1 1/2 cups spaghetti sauce
12 cooked lasagna noodles
Non-stick cooking spray

PREPARATION

In a medium bowl, combine tofu, 1 cup cheese, eggs, spinach, parsley, basil, salt, pepper and nutmeg.

Spray a 9x13-inch baking dish with non-stick cooking spray. Spread 1/2 cup spaghetti sauce in baking dish. Top with 4 noodles, half of the tofu mixture and repeat. Top with remaining 4 noodles, remaining spaghetti sauce and 1 cup cheese. Bake at 350 degrees F. for 35 minutes.

Vegetable Lasagna

4 to 6 servings

INGREDIENTS

Carrot Layer:
2 tablespoons olive oil
1 onion
1 lb. carrots
1 (15 oz.) carton reduced fat ricotta cheese, divided
Salt and pepper to taste

Spinach Layer:
2 (10 oz. each) pkg. frozen spinach
1 tablespoon olive oil
2 green onions, chopped
1 egg

Eggplant and Zucchini Layer:
1 medium zucchini, sliced
1 medium eggplant, cut into 1/8-inch thick slices
6 tablespoons olive oil, divided
3 garlic cloves

1 lb. lasagna noodles
2 1/2 cups tomato sauce
4 tablespoons fresh basil, chopped
4 cups grated cheese
3 cups Parmesan cheese
Non-stick cooking spray

PREPARATION

Carrot Layer: Sauté onions and carrots in olive oil; drain. Puree in food processor with 1/2 of the ricotta cheese. Add salt and pepper.

Spinach Layer: Cook spinach according to package directions. Drain, cool and squeeze out water. Place in food processor. Heat oil, sauté green onions and add along with ricotta and egg to processor and puree.

Eggplant and Zucchini Layer: Salt zucchini and eggplant; place between paper towels. Let stand 30 minutes. Heat 2 tablespoons oil and 1 minced garlic clove in a heavy pan over medium heat. Add eggplant and zucchini in a single layer. Cook until tender and golden, turning occasionally (about 10 minutes for eggplant); transfer to paper towels to drain. Repeat with remaining oil, garlic and eggplant/zucchini in 2 more batches. Season with pepper.

Cook noodles according to package directions. Drain and rinse with cold water; drain. Spray a 9x13-inch baking dish with non-stick cooking spray. Spread 3/4 cup tomato sauce on bottom of dish. Arrange 1/4 of noodles over sauce.
Spread carrot puree. Ladle 1/2 cup tomato sauce over carrot puree. Sprinkle with 1 cup mozzarella cheese, 1 tablespoon basil and 1/4 cup Parmesan cheese.

Top with 1/4 of the noodles. Season with pepper. Spread spinach mixture over noodles. Spread 1/2 cup tomato sauce on top. Sprinkle with 1 cup mozzarella cheese, 1 tablespoon basil and 1/4 cup Parmesan cheese.

Top with 1/4 of the noodles. Season with pepper. Arrange overlapping slices of eggplant and zucchini. Spread with 1/2 cup tomato sauce. Sprinkle with remaining basil, mozzarella and Parmesan cheeses. Bake at 350 degrees F. about 1 hour and 15 minutes, or until heated through and bubbly. Cool 10 minutes before serving.

Pork Chops with Spaghetti

4 servings

INGREDIENTS

3 tablespoons extra-virgin olive oil
1/2 cup butter, melted, divided
2 large garlic cloves, mashed
1/3 teaspoon freshly ground black pepper
1/8 teaspoon of crushed red pepper (optional)
4 lean pork chops, 1 inch thick
1 teaspoon crumbled dried rosemary
1/2 teaspoon salt
4 medium-sized ripe tomatoes or 2 cups canned peeled Italian tomatoes, chopped
10 fresh parsley sprigs, leaves only, chopped
3/4 lb. spaghetti
1/4 cup Parmesan cheese, grated

PREPARATION

Combine olive oil and 1/4 cup of butter in a large heavy skillet and heat. Add garlic and black and red pepper and cook slowly for 2 minutes. Add pork chops, sprinkle with rosemary, and brown on each side for 5 minutes. Lower heat to medium and add salt, tomatoes and parsley. Cover and cook slowly for 20 minutes.

Uncover and cook slowly for 20 minutes longer, or until done. Place spaghetti in a large pot of boiling salted water. Cook for about 10 minutes; drain well. Place back in the pot in which it was cooked. Add remaining 1/4 cup butter and mix well. Add grated cheese and a little sauce from the pork chops and mix.

Place spaghetti on a hot plate with pork chops and pour sauce over both.

Thin Noodles with Ricotta

6 servings

INGREDIENTS

1 lb. thin, narrow egg noodles
3/4 cup heavy cream
2 cups (1 lb.) fresh ricotta, whole or skim milk
1 tablespoon olive oil
Salt
Freshly ground white or black pepper
2 or 3 drops of Tabasco, or to taste (optional)
1 cup Parmesan cheese, grated

PREPARATION

Cook noodles in 6 quarts rapidly boiling salted water until barely al dente; about 5 to 8 minutes.

While noodles are cooking, heat cream in a heavy saucepan but do not boil. Stir in ricotta. Stir with a wooden spoon or wire whip until ricotta and cream are blended into a creamy mixture. Stir in olive oil, salt and pepper to taste, Tabasco and 1/2 cup Parmesan cheese. Mix well. Keep very hot without boiling.

Drain pasta and pour into a heated deep serving dish. Add sauce and remaining Parmesan; toss well. Serve immediately on hot plates.

 # Pasta Soups

Chicken Noodle Soup

6 to 8 servings

INGREDIENTS

12 cups water
10 chicken bouillon cubes
3 chicken breasts
4 carrots, sliced or grated
2 tablespoons dried minced onion or 1 whole onion, diced
2 tablespoons parsley
Salt and pepper to taste
4 oz. wide egg noodles
2 oz. macaroni

PREPARATION

In a large saucepan or Dutch oven, bring water, bouillon, chicken, carrots, onion and parsley to a boil. Lower heat and simmer for 1 hour.

When chicken is tender remove from saucepan, cool and cut into bite-size pieces. Return meat to saucepan, add salt and pepper, macaroni, noodles. Simmer 30 minutes or until noodles are done.

Optionally, celery and rice can be added.

Pasta Fagioli (Gravy Version)

4 servings

INGREDIENTS

2 ham hocks
1 (16 oz.) bag cranberry beans
6 potatoes, cubed
3 carrots, sliced
1 stalk celery, sliced
1 lb. bacon, chopped
3 tablespoons flour
1 cup elbow macaroni

PREPARATION

Place beans and ham hocks in a 5 quart Dutch oven. Cover with water and cook beans until soft, about 1 1/2 to 2 hours. Add potatoes, carrots and celery and cook until tender.

Fry bacon until almost burnt; remove bacon from grease. Add flour to bacon grease and thicken. Add flour mixture to soup with bacon.

Cook pasta according to directions on package; drain. Add cooked macaroni to soup. Heat and serve.

Vegetable-Noodle Soup with Garlic

6 to 8 servings

INGREDIENTS

1/4 cup butter
1 large onion, sliced
3 potatoes, sliced
2 large ripe tomatoes, peeled and chopped
6 to 7 cups beef stock*
1/8 cup chopped parsley
1/8 teaspoon oregano
Salt and pepper to taste
1 cup green beans, sliced
1/4 cup vermicelli, broken into small pieces
2 to 3 cloves garlic, peeled and crushed
3 sprigs fresh basil or 2 teaspoons dried basil
2 slices tomatoes, broiled
Grated Parmesan cheese

PREPARATION

Melt butter in large saucepan. Add onion and potatoes; sauté gently for 5 to 6 minutes, without browning. Add 2 large tomatoes and sauté for 1 minute longer.

Add beef stock and bring to a boil. Add parsley and oregano, salt, pepper, beans, and vermicelli. Cook over low heat for about 10 minutes or until beans and noodles are tender.

Meanwhile, prepare garlic paste by mixing crushed garlic with basil and broiled tomato slices. Pound all together to make smooth paste, adding a little soup broth to moisten. Just before serving, add garlic paste to soup and mix well. Serve hot with grated cheese in a separate dish.

Beef stock/broth recipe page 162

Vegetable Chicken Soup

Stewing hens are used in soup because of their superior nutrient value at a low cost. Stewing hens will need to be cooked at a low heat for an hour or more before becoming tender. Stewing hens will provide plenty of delicious meat and tasty chicken stock.

4 servings

INGREDIENTS

1/2 stewing chicken, about 1-1/2 lbs.
1 1/2 teaspoons salt
6 whole peppercorns
1 stalk celery
1 carrot
1 large onion
1 clove garlic, peeled
1 tomato, quartered
1/2 cup shelled peas
1/2 cup cauliflower florets
1/2 cup celery, julienned
1/2 cup carrots, julienned
1/2 cup vermicelli

PREPARATION

Place chicken in a large pot, cover with cold water, and bring to a boil; skim as needed. Add salt, peppercorns, celery stalk, carrot, onion, garlic, and tomato to chicken; reduce heat and cook for 1 hour. Remove chicken from stock. Remove skin and bones; dice chicken meat.

Place peas, cauliflower florets, and julienne strips of celery and carrot in a large saucepan with 1 cup water; boil for 10 minutes. Drain vegetables and set aside.

Cook vermicelli for 3 minutes in 2 cups boiling water; drain.

Combine diced chicken, vermicelli and vegetables in a soup tureen or serving bowl. Strain stock into tureen and serve.

Winter Vegetable Soup with Pasta

4 servings

INGREDIENTS

1 tablespoon olive oil
1 large onion, chopped
1 small rutabaga, peeled and thickly sliced
1 cup sliced celery
1 cup sliced carrots
1/4 head white cabbage, shredded
4 cups hot beef broth*
1/2 cup vermicelli
1 tablespoon chopped parsley
1/4 cup low fat sour cream, optional

PREPARATION

Heat olive oil in a large saucepan. Add onions and sauté until translucent. Add rutabaga, celery, carrots and cabbage; sauté for 1 minute longer.

Add beef broth and simmer, covered, for 20 minutes. Add vermicelli; stir and cook for about 4 minutes, or until pasta is just tender. Serve each portion garnished with chopped parsley and 1 tablespoon sour cream, if desired.

*Beef stock/broth recipe page 162

Italian Wedding Soup

6 servings

INGREDIENTS

2 teaspoons olive oil
1 garlic clove, diced
1/2 cup onion, finely chopped
1 cup bell pepper, red, diced
2 cups zucchini, diced
2 cups yellow summer squash, diced
3 (14.5 oz.) cans chicken broth*
5 oz. (1 cup) elbow macaroni or ditalini
2 cups spinach, fresh, coarsely chopped
Parmesan cheese

PREPARATION

In large, heavy pot, sauté garlic and onion in olive oil. Stir in bell pepper, zucchini and summer squash; sauté until tender-crisp.

Stir in chicken broth and elbow macaroni. Increase heat. When soup boils, reduce heat and simmer until pasta is tender, stirring occasionally. Add spinach; cook until wilted. Spoon soup into individual bowls and garnish with Parmesan cheese.

Chicken stock/broth recipe page 164

Minestrone Soup

6 servings

INGREDIENTS

2 cups (1 lb.) dry, small red beans
2 quarts water + 1 1/2 cups water, divided
1 (28 oz. can) peeled whole tomatoes and juice
2 cup onion, chopped
1 1/2 cups carrots, shredded
1 cup celery, finely-chopped
2 garlic cloves, crushed
2 teaspoons salt
1/4 teaspoon pepper
2 cups cabbage, shredded
1 (6 oz. can) tomato paste
1/2 cup rigatoni

PREPARATION

Combine beans and 2 quarts water in a 6-quart covered pot. Heat to boiling and cook for 2 minutes; remove from heat. Cover and let stand for 1 hour. Stir in tomatoes with juice, onion, carrots, celery, garlic, salt and pepper. Break up tomatoes, then bring to boil. Reduce heat, cover and simmer until beans are tender (about 2 hours). Stir in cabbage, remaining 1 1/2 cups water, tomato paste and rigatoni. Boil gently, covered, 20 minutes, or until rigatoni is done.

Sausage Minestrone

Yield = 2 ½ quarts

INGREDIENTS

1/2 pound bulk Italian sausage
1 cup onion, chopped
2 cloves garlic, minced
8 cups water
1 (28 oz.) can Italian-style tomatoes, broken, undrained
5 teaspoons beef-flavor instant bouillon or 5 cubes
4 teaspoons Italian seasoning
1/4 teaspoon pepper
2 medium carrots, sliced
1 (15.5 oz.) can garbanzo beans, drained
1 (9 oz.) pkg. frozen cut green beans, thawed
8 oz. uncooked spaghetti, broken
Parmesan cheese

PREPARATION

In large kettle or Dutch oven, brown sausage, onion and garlic; drain. Add water, tomatoes, bouillon, Italian seasoning, pepper and carrots; bring to a boil.

Reduce heat; simmer uncovered 1 hour. Stir in beans and spaghetti; bring to a boil. Reduce heat; simmer uncovered 10 minutes or until spaghetti and green beans are tender. Serve with Parmesan cheese.

Italian Minestrone

10 servings

INGREDIENTS

1 cup dried navy beans
2 cups beef bouillon
6 cups water
1 large onion, chopped
1 clove garlic, minced
3 large carrots, diced
3 stalks celery with leaves, diced
1 cup potatoes, chopped
2 tablespoons olive oil
1/2 cup elbow macaroni
1 teaspoon salt
1/4 teaspoon pepper
1 cup cooked or canned tomatoes

PREPARATION

Place beans, bouillon and water in stock pot; cook 3 to 4 hours.

Sauté onion, garlic, carrots, celery and potatoes in olive oil. Add sautéed vegetables to beans; cook slowly 30 minutes, stirring often. Add macaroni, salt, pepper and tomatoes to soup; simmer 15 minutes. If thinner consistency is desired, add more water.

Tortellini Soup

6 servings

INGREDIENTS

3 tablespoons butter
1 small onion, chopped
2 cloves garlic, minced
2 medium stalks celery, chopped
1 medium carrot, chopped
8 cups chicken broth*
4 cups water
2 (10 oz.) pkg. uncooked cheese-filled tortellini
2 tablespoons fresh parsley, chopped
1 teaspoon freshly-grated nutmeg
1/2 teaspoon pepper
Parmesan cheese

PREPARATION

In a heavy covered 6-quart pot, melt butter and sauté onion, garlic, celery and carrot; add chicken broth and water. Heat to boiling: reduce heat and add tortellini. Simmer, covered, for 20 minutes, stirring occasionally, or tortellini is tender. Add parsley, nutmeg and pepper. Cover and cook 10 minutes. Garnish individual servings with Parmesan cheese.

*Chicken stock/broth recipe page 164

Italian Stew

4 servings

INGREDIENTS

2 lb. lean stew meat, cut into 1 1/2-inch cubes
1 tablespoon flour
3 tablespoons olive oil
2 cloves garlic, minced
3 large onions, quartered
1 cup beef broth*
2 tablespoons seasoned salt
1 teaspoon chili powder
1 teaspoon dried oregano
1 teaspoon dried rosemary
1 (6 oz.) can tomato paste
2 (14.5 oz. each) cans Italian stewed tomatoes
1/2 cup fresh parsley, minced
3 medium carrots, cut into 1-inch pieces
8 oz. mostaccioli or penne pasta
1/3 cup Parmesan cheese

PREPARATION

Coat meat with flour; brown in 3 tablespoons oil in a 5-quart Dutch oven. Add garlic and onions, sautéing until tender. Stir in beef broth, salt, chili powder, oregano and rosemary. Cover and simmer 10 minutes.

Add tomato paste, stewed tomatoes, parsley and carrots. Cover and simmer 1 hour, or until meat is tender.

Cook pasta according to package directions; drain. Stir pasta into Dutch oven and heat through. Sprinkle servings with Parmesan.

Beef stock/broth recipe page 162

 # Salads & Sides

Vermicelli Salad with Crabmeat

4 servings

INGREDIENTS

8 oz. vermicelli
8 black Chinese dried mushrooms
1 lb. crabmeat
4 scallions, sliced
1 cup water chestnuts, drained and cut into thin strips
1 cup bamboo shoots, drained and cut into thin strips
2 tablespoons soy sauce
2 tablespoons sweet and sour sauce
3 drops hot chili sauce
3 tablespoons oil
3 tablespoons lemon juice

PREPARATION

Cook pasta according to package directions until al dente; drain.

Place mushrooms in bowl and cover with boiling water; let soak for 30 minutes. Drain and cut into strips.

In a large bowl, combine pasta, mushrooms, crabmeat, scallions, water chestnuts, bamboo shoots, soy sauce, sweet and sour sauce, chili sauce, and oil; mix well. Sprinkle salad with lemon juice, and serve.

Garden Pasta Salad

8 servings

INGREDIENTS

2 cups rotini
1 1/2 cups small broccoli flowerets
1 cup tomato, diced
1 small zucchini, thinly sliced
1/2 cup black olives, sliced
1/2 cup green bell pepper, chopped
1/2 cup red onion, chopped
1/2 cup Parmesan cheese

Dressing:

2/3 cup olive oil
1/3 cup red wine vinegar
1 teaspoon dry mustard
1 garlic clove, crushed
Salt and pepper to taste

PREPARATION

Cook pasta according to package directions; rinse and drain. Mix pasta with broccoli, tomato, zucchini, black olives, bell pepper, onion and Parmesan cheese. Blend oil, vinegar, mustard, garlic, salt and pepper in a small container. Toss with salad; chill before serving.

The Best Macaroni and Cheese

8 to 10 servings

INGREDIENTS

2 cups elbow macaroni
2 cups low fat small-curd cottage cheese
1 cup low fat sour cream
12 oz. sharp Cheddar cheese, shredded
8 oz. reduced fat mozzarella cheese, shredded
1 egg, beaten
1 cup milk
1 1/2 teaspoons salt
1/8 teaspoon black pepper to taste
1/8 teaspoon paprika to taste

PREPARATION

Cook pasta according to package directions; drain.

Blend cottage cheese, sour cream, Cheddar cheese, mozzarella cheese, egg, milk, salt and pepper in a large bowl. Stir in the macaroni. Spray a 9x13-inch baking dish with non-stick cooking spray; add macaroni mixture. Sprinkle with paprika. Bake at 350 degrees F. for 45 to 60 minutes or until brown.

Rotini Salad

6 servings

INGREDIENTS

10 to 16 oz. rotini
1 cup vegetables, cut into bite-size pieces
1 medium onion, chopped
1 cucumber, quartered and sliced
1 green bell pepper, chopped
1 small jar pimientos
1 stalk of celery, chopped

Dressing:
1 cup cider vinegar
1 cup granulated sugar
2 teaspoons salt
2 teaspoons pepper
2 teaspoons garlic salt
1 tablespoon dry mustard
3 tablespoons parsley flakes
2 teaspoon Accent

PREPARATION

Cook pasta according to package directions; drain, rinse with cold water.

Blend together dressing ingredients: vinegar, sugar, salt, pepper, garlic salt, dry mustard, parsley and Accent in a small bowl.

Mix vegetables, onion, cucumber, bell pepper, pimentos and celery with pasta in a large container. Toss with vinegar dressing and chill before serving.

Broccoli Tortellini Salad

6 servings

INGREDIENTS

1 (7 oz.) pkg. cheese tortellini
1 cup broccoli, loosely chopped
1/2 cup fresh parsley, finely chopped
1 teaspoon pimiento, chopped
1 (6 oz.) jar artichoke hearts, marinated and undrained
2 1/2 teaspoons fresh basil, chopped or 1/4 teaspoon dried basil
2 green onions, sliced
1/2 teaspoon garlic powder
1/2 cup reduced fat Italian dressing
5 to 6 cherry or grape tomatoes, cut in half
¼ cup Parmesan cheese
Black olives, sliced

PREPARATION

Cook pasta according to directions on package; rinse and drain.

Mix together all ingredients, except tomatoes, cheese and olives. Refrigerate, covered, for 4 to 6 hours. Before serving, add tomatoes and toss. Garnish with olives and Parmesan cheese.

Special Tuna Salad

4 servings

INGREDIENTS

2 cups macaroni
2 cups cucumbers, sliced
1 1/2 cups tomatoes, diced
1 (7 oz.) can tuna, drained
1/4 cup green bell pepper, sliced
1/4 cup celery, diced
1/4 cup onion, diced
1 cup light mayonnaise
1/2 cup light Italian dressing
1 teaspoon dill weed
1 tablespoon prepared yellow mustard
1 teaspoon salt
1/4 teaspoon pepper

PREPARATION

Cook pasta according to directions on package; rinse in cold water and drain. In a large bowl, combine cucumbers, tomatoes, tuna, bell pepper, celery and onion with macaroni.

Dressing: In a small bowl, blend mayonnaise, Italian dressing, dill weed, mustard, salt and pepper. Toss macaroni with dressing and chill.

Everlasting Salad

4 servings

INGREDIENTS

1 (7 oz.) pkg. elbow macaroni
1 (15 oz.) can crushed pineapple, drained
8 large apples, chopped (unpeeled)
1 lb. miniature marshmallows
1 cup granulated sugar
4 eggs, beaten
2 lemons
2 tablespoons flour
1 pint whipping cream or non-fat dairy whipped topping

PREPARATION

Cook pasta according to package directions; rinse, drain and cool. Combine macaroni, pineapple, apples and marshmallows; set aside.

In a double boiler, cook sugar, eggs, juice of lemons and flour until thick. Let cool and pour over fruit and pasta mixture. Let stand in refrigerator overnight. Before serving, whip cream and fold into salad.

Sweet and Sour Salad

6 servings

INGREDIENTS

8 oz. elbow macaroni
1 medium green or red bell pepper, chopped
1/2 medium cucumber, sliced
1 medium onion, coarsely chopped

Dressing:
1 cup cider vinegar
3/4 cup granulated sugar
1 teaspoon parsley flakes
1 1/2 teaspoons salt
1 teaspoon garlic powder
1/4 teaspoon pepper

PREPARATION

Cook pasta according to package directions; rinse with cold water, drain and pour into large bowl. Add peppers, cucumber and onion.

To make dressing, combine the remaining ingredients in a jar with lid. Shake until sugar is dissolved. Pour over salad, toss and chill.

Cheese Tortellini Pasta Salad

4 to 6 servings

INGREDIENTS

2 1/2 cups cherry tomatoes, sliced
2 cups snow peas
2 cups fresh mushrooms
2 cups broccoli
1 (6 oz.) can black olives, drained and sliced
1 (8 oz.) pkg. cheese tortellini
3 oz. fettuccini
1 tablespoon Parmesan cheese

Dressing:

1/2 cup green onions
1/3 cup red wine vinegar
1/3 cup olive oil
1/3 cup vegetable oil
2 tablespoons parsley
2 cloves garlic
2 teaspoons basil
1 teaspoon dill weed
1 teaspoon salt
1/2 teaspoon pepper
1/2 teaspoon granulated sugar
1/2 teaspoon oregano
1 1/2 teaspoons Dijon mustard

PREPARATION

Blanch snow peas and broccoli for 1 minute. Drain and cool. In a large bowl, combine tomatoes, peas, mushrooms, broccoli and black olives. Cook pasta according to package directions; drain and cool. Add vegetables to pasta and add cheese.

Dressing: Combine ingredients in a jar and shake vigorously. Toss with pasta mixture. Chill at least 4 hours.

Sweet and Sour Pasta Salad

4 servings

INGREDIENTS

8 oz. spaghetti
1/4 cup corn oil
2 tablespoons sesame oil
1/2 teaspoon dry crushed red pepper
3 tablespoons honey
2 tablespoons soy sauce
1 teaspoon salt
2 tablespoons chopped cilantro
1/4 cup chopped roasted peanuts
1/4 cup green onion (chopped)
1 tablespoon toasted sesame seeds

PREPARATION

Cook spaghetti according to package directions. Rinse pasta in cool water and drain.

Microwave together corn oil, sesame oil and dry crushed red pepper flakes until hot and fragrant. Add honey, soy sauce and salt. Mix in cilantro, peanuts, chopped onion and sesame seeds. Toss cooked pasta with cooled dressing.

Healthy Substitutions for Canned Soup

Most busy cooks use shortcuts whenever they can. Those cans of condensed soup and broth save loads of time when dinner has to be ready in a hurry. But by making your own broths and cream soups, you have more control of the amount of sodium and fat in your family's diet.

Plus, the homemade flavor just can't be beat!

Homemade Vegetable Stock

Here's a way to use up all those leftover vegetable pieces. Make a healthy stock with them! (Bell peppers, pea pods, onions, mushrooms, carrots, corn cobs, potato parings, etc.) Stock freezes well, so use what you need and freeze the rest for later.

3 medium carrots
2 potatoes
1 large onion
2 stalks celery
2 tomatoes
All saved vegetable leftovers
2 quarts cold water
1/2 cup fresh parsley, chopped
1 teaspoon thyme or 5 sprigs fresh thyme
1 bay leaf
1/2 teaspoon salt
1/8 teaspoon black pepper

Wash vegetables and cut into 1-inch pieces. Place in large stock pot with leftover vegetables. Fill pot with 2 quarts cold water and bring to a boil. Add parsley, thyme, bay leaf, salt and pepper. Reduce heat and simmer partially covered for 45 minutes to an hour.

Strain stock through a colander lined with cheesecloth or a clean tea towel and discard vegetables. Store in refrigerator for up to one week or freeze in an airtight container for up to 6 months.

Homemade Cream of Mushroom Soup

1/2 cup fresh mushroom caps, sliced thin
3 tablespoons butter
1/4 cup corn starch
4 cups 1% or 2% milk, divided
1 teaspoon sea salt
1/8 teaspoon black pepper

In a medium saucepan over medium heat, sauté mushrooms in butter until mushrooms are tender. In a medium bowl, whisk together corn starch and 1 1/2 cups of milk. Whisk or stir corn starch mixture into saucepan with mushrooms; slowly add remaining milk, salt and pepper. Stir over medium heat until smooth and thick.

Homemade Beef Stock or Broth

Classic beef stock begins by slowly roasting the soup bones, a process that will caramelize the bones. Alternatively, you can also caramelize the bones in 1 to 2 tablespoons of vegetable oil over medium-high heat in a large saucepan (in batches) for a few minutes on each side. Using this method is faster, but the hot fat will splatter. After removing the bones from the saucepan, drain most of the excess fat, add a little water, add carrots and onion and cook until browned.

A real bone stock is made with bones and cuts of meat high in collagen, like marrow, feet and knuckles but any bones can be used.

To make **homemade beef broth,** use the same recipe as for stock but add meat in with the bones or use meaty soup bones such as short ribs or beef shanks and leave the meat on the bones for more flavor. Beef broth and stock are interchangeable in most recipes. Broth is made with more actual meat versus the stripped bones used for beef stock.

6 lbs. beef soup bones
3 large carrots
1 medium onion
2 celery stalks (especially the tops)
1 medium potato
1 large tomato

2 cloves garlic
2 bay leaves
1 teaspoon salt
1/4 teaspoon black pepper
Water

Blanching - This step, to be done before roasting and cooking, removes the impurities from the bones. To blanch, cover the bones with cold water, bring to a boil, and let them cook at an aggressive simmer for 20 minutes before draining and roasting.

Roasting - Wash carrots and chop into 1-inch pieces. Cut onion into chunks. In a shallow roasting pan, place carrots, onion and soup bones. Bake at 450 degrees F. for 30 minutes or until bones are well browned, turning occasionally.

Drain fat. Add 1/2 cup water to roasting pan with soup bones; pour all into a large stock pot.

Wash and roughly chop celery, potato (with peel) and tomato into large pieces. Add celery, potato, tomato, garlic, bay leaves, salt and pepper to stock pot. Pour in just enough cold water to cover, bring to a boil, reduce heat to a simmer, and cover.

Skim any fat and foam from the surface of the water. Simmer for 3 to 5 hours. Strain stock through a fine-mesh sieve into a shallow, wide container, pressing on solids; discard solids. Let the finished broth cool slowly before transferring to refrigerator.

Homemade Chicken Stock or Broth

If making chicken stock for freezing, you may want to simmer the stock for an hour or so longer, making it more concentrated and easier to store. Stock can also be made in a slow cooker.

When making stock, remember the flavor is derived from the bones, not the meat on the bones.

To make **homemade chicken broth**, use the same recipe as for chicken stock but add meat in with the bones or use meaty bones for more flavor. Chicken broth and stock are interchangeable in most recipes. Broth is made with more actual chicken versus the stripped bones used for chicken stock.

Leftover bones and skin from a chicken carcass
2 celery stalks (especially the tops)
1 medium onion
1 or 2 carrots
1 teaspoon salt
1/4 teaspoon black pepper
1 bay leaf
2 fresh parsley sprigs

Chop celery, onion and carrots into large pieces. Using a large stock pot, add chicken bones, skin, celery, onion and carrots. Cover with cold water. Add salt, pepper, bay leaf and parsley. Bring to a boil; reduce heat to simmer. Simmer, partially covered, for 4 hours or more, using a slotted spoon to remove any foam from the surface.

Remove and discard bones, skin and vegetables. Strain stock through a colander lined with cheesecloth or a clean tea towel, or a fine-meshed sieve. Cool quickly in refrigerator.

Homemade Cream of Chicken Soup

1 1/2 cups chicken stock (see chicken stock recipe page)
1 teaspoon onion, finely chopped
1 clove garlic, finely chopped
1 1/2 cups 1% or 2% milk, divided
1/4 teaspoon sea salt
1/8 teaspoon black pepper
1/4 teaspoon fresh parsley, chopped
1/8 teaspoon ground allspice
1/8 teaspoon ground paprika
1/8 teaspoon lemon pepper seasoning
3/4 cup all-purpose flour

In a large saucepan over medium heat, add 1 tablespoon chicken stock, onion and garlic. Cook 3 minutes or until softened. Pour in remaining chicken stock and 1/2 cup milk. Whisk in salt, pepper, parsley, allspice, paprika and lemon pepper. Bring to a boil, reduce heat and simmer for 1 to 2 minutes.

In a medium bowl, whisk together flour and 1 cup of milk until smooth. Whisk milk mixture into stock mixture. Continue whisking (to avoid lumps) until soup thickens and almost comes to a boil.

Hey, if you loved this book and want to get more freebies and recipes like these, subscribe to the newsletter at:

http://www.BonnieScottAuthor.com/subscribe.html

Also by Bonnie Scott

  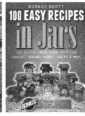  

Cookie Indulgence – 150 Easy Cookie Recipes

4 Ingredient Cookbook: 150 Quick Timesaving Recipes

100 Easy Recipes in Jars

Chocolate Bliss: 150 Easy Chocolate Recipes

100 Easy Camping Recipes

View more of my books at my Amazon Author Page - https://www.amazon.com/Bonnie-Scott/e/B008MM40AY

Made in the USA
Las Vegas, NV
15 December 2024